Don't Break Your Heart
Cookbook

Don't Break Your Heart
Cookbook

Shara Aaron, MS, RD and Monica Bearden, RD

Race Point
PUBLISHING

A division of Book Sales, Inc.
276 Fifth Avenue Suite 206
New York, New York 10001

RACE POINT PUBLISHING and the distinctive Race Point Publishing logo
are trademarks of Book Sales, Inc.

© 2013 by The Book Shop, Ltd.
7 Peter Cooper Road
New York, NY 10010

This 2013 edition published by Race Point Publishing by arrangement with
The Book Shop, Ltd.

Photo Credits: Lew Robertson/Getty Images: Front Cover; iStockphoto/Thinkstock: Front Endpaper, 1, 3, 5, 6, 8, 10, 12, 14, 16, 20, 22, 24, 27, 29, 30, 31, 33, 35, 36, 38, 47, 52, 53, 55, 60, 65, 66, 69, 72, 74, 77, 78, 79, 80, 83, 85, 86, 89, 90, 91, 93, 94, 95, 96, 97, 98, 104, 109, 111, 112, 119, 122, 124, 125, 126, 128, 131, 134, 137, 139, 140, 143, 145, 148, 150, 151, 153, 155, 156, 158, 159, 160, 161, 162, 163, 165, 166, 168, 171, 172, 174, 175, 178, 179, 181, 183, 185, 194, 196, 200, 202, 205, 206, 207, 208, 209, 210, 213, 214, 215, 216, 217, 218, 220, 221, 223, 224, 226, 227, 228, 229, 237, 240, 241, 242, 243, 244, 245, 246, 248, 250, 251, 253, 257, 258, 260, 261, 264, 266, 268, 271, 277, 278, 279, 280, 281, 282, 283, Back Cover; National Pork Board: 43, 44, 48, 51; Texas Beef Council: 57, 58; National Chicken Council: 103; Camille Macres: 107, 108, 151, 186, 190, 193, 201; National Turkey Federation: 115; The Almond Board of California: 272, 275; Courtesy of the Authors: 288; Zoonar/Thinkstock: Back Endpaper

EDITOR Catherine Nichols
DESIGN AND PHOTO RESEARCH Tim Palin Creative

ISBN-13: 978-1-937994-14-3

Printed in China

2 4 6 8 10 9 7 5 3 1

www.racepointpub.com

Contents

Introduction

It's simple really: eat healthy and you will live longer, better. Critiqued by a panel of foodies, real people, and health experts, this collection of recipes is designed to make heart-healthy cooking both easy and delicious. All our recipes feature ingredients that support heart health and the enjoyment of food. This is not your typical "healthy" cookbook. You won't have to sacrifice taste for health. Instead, you are introduced to the true joy of eating rich and tantalizing foods that not only delight the palate, but your whole being. By eating the right foods, you will feel energetic, spirited, wholesome, and powerful. There is nothing more empowering than taking care of yourself and providing a good example to those around you. An added bonus-- eating better will lead to looking better and having more energy.

Each chapter starts with quick facts about the ingredients and foods highlighted in the coming pages. Next, the featured nutrients and health information for those ingredients are listed. The recipes in this book offer a wide assortment of flavorful dishes that are both heart-healthy and easy to prepare. Each recipe is accompanied by a nutritional analysis, with specific nutrients highlighted for those recipes providing exceptional amounts of your daily needs.

chapter 1

Success Starts Here

Feel great, look great, and enjoy your food: that is the goal for this book. The information presented in each chapter can increase your level of healthful food know-how and be the start to a whole new way of eating. Think of this cookbook as an adventure in cuisine that can lead to a better you. Learn about heart-healthy cooking and ingredients so that eating healthy becomes second nature. Studies show that those who eat healthfully lead healthier lives as a whole. Your newfound interest in wholesome ingredients and taking care of yourself will not only give you a more energetic and active lifestyle but will also impact those around you.

A Heart-Healthy Lifestyle

Healthful ingredients can help decrease chronic inflammation and chronic stress hormones that wreak havoc on your body and how you feel. Eating healthier and taking the time to focus on what you put in your body is a big step in the right direction to eliminating the stressors that wear down your vascular health. By maintaining healthy vessels and blood flow you are impacting your whole self – from outward beauty, like better hair, skin, and nails, to healthier internal systems like the heart, eyes, brain, liver, and kidneys. Research shows that certain foods not only help to take care of your vessels but can actually reverse damage. This cookbook uses those ingredients shown to benefit your vessels.

Along with making changes in your diet, there are other lifestyle changes to be considered. It is easy to get in ruts, even healthful ruts, like eating the same foods and doing the same exercises. Change things up a bit and try something new. If you do not exercise, start walking and jumping rope. If you do exercise, add yoga or Pilates to your routine. Variety is key to everything you do, including the foods you choose and how you live your life. Stepping out of the monotony of routine adds spice to your life and can lead to a healthier lifestyle. For example, research shows that changing your daily routine is good for keeping a sharp mind. Additionally, changing your workout routine helps "shock" your body into a leaner and stronger you. So, here are some tips for success:

- ♥ **Cook healthfully.** Eating out increases your fat and salt intake by as much as 40 percent, so cook at home using nutritious ingredients. This book will help show you how.

- ♥ **Get moving.** All exercise counts towards maintaining a healthy heart, strong muscles and bones, and maintaining healthy blood sugar, cholesterol, and triglyceride levels.

- ♥ **Get enough sleep.** At least 7 to 8 hours a night will help decrease stress hormones that lead to belly fat and clogged vessels.

- ♥ **Calm down.** Try and decrease the stressors in your life. Say no to extra responsibilities and focus on what is most important in your life.

- ♥ **Find passion.** Make sure to have plenty of time and energy for your passions. Being passionate about life and what you do will keep you healthy and happy.

- ♥ **Pick your friends wisely.** Being a part of a group, a healthy group, is good for you. Research shows that a friend's eating habits can affect your waistline. Also, when people have a workout buddy, they exercise longer and tend to stick with it.

Because we are not just dietitians, but foodies as well as moms, this book is chock full of real advice and real food for real people. For this reason, all the guidelines are based on recommendations given by credible sources such as the American Heart Association (AHA), the United States Department of Agriculture (USDA) Dietary Guidelines, the Food and Nutrition Board of the Institute of Medicine of the National Academies Dietary Reference Intakes, the USDA Food Database, the National Institutes of Health Office of Dietary Supplements, as well as published research in reputable journals.

Each recipe in this book is compared to the guidelines set by the agencies listed above. Occasionally, a recipe contains more total fat than the AHA guidelines. That's because public health guidelines tend to focus more on total fat rather than the quality of the fat. Recent research, however, indicates that the type of fat matters more than the quantity.

And, in fact, a diet rich in healthy, plant-based, unsaturated fats can be very healthy for your cardiovascular system. This book reflects this research. The recipes feature all the quality foods and ingredients shown to take care of your cardiovascular health. This includes borrowing from the Mediterranean diet. Two of the guidelines that all recipes adhere to are the sodium and cholesterol criteria listed below.

- No more than ⅖ teaspoon (480 mg) of sodium for a side dish and no more than ¼ teaspoon (600 mg) of sodium for an entree.

- No more than ⅙ teaspoon (300 mg) of cholesterol for a side dish or entree.

These criteria are based on the American Heart Association guidelines as well as the FDA definition of "healthy" for labeling foods.

When evaluating how you eat, your total diet is the primary consideration. Criteria to evaluate any individual meal or food is tricky and can be misleading. For example, you may find a whole grain recipe to be high in carbohydrates, even though they are good carbohydrates, and a recipe with nuts to be high in fat, even though it is good fat. Should you exclude these recipes from your diet? Not necessarily. Adding healthful ingredients to your meals benefits your overall well-being. Instead, pay attention to the broader dietary guidelines when considering a healthy lifestyle.

Based on the recommendations from the Food and Nutrition Board, adults should get 45 percent to 65 percent of their calories from carbohydrates, 15 percent to 35 percent from protein, and 20 percent to 35 percent from fat. This represents the macronutrient breakdown of your food and is indicated in the nutritional boxes provided for all of the recipes included in this book.

Try to follow the following guidelines when considering your diet:

- Focus on healthy fats with up to 15 percent monounsaturated and 10 percent polyunsaturated. Limit yourself to no more than 10 percent saturated fat.

- Aim for 25 to 38 grams of fiber daily, making sure to drink plenty of water when increasing your fiber intake.

- Limit your cholesterol to 300 milligrams and your sodium intake to 2,300 milligrams per day.

chapter 2

Incredible Ingredients

Incredible ingredients will make your meals just that, incredible. They will keep you healthy and make your foods delicious. Incredible ingredients are foods, beverages, spices, and herbs that are both nutritional and flavor powerhouses. Yes, you can have both: nutrition and great taste. Adding the foods listed below to your diet boosts not only the heart-healthy nutrients of each meal, but also flavor and enjoyment. With today's understanding of our food supply and its impact on our health, we are able to bring you this list of "incredible ingredients."

Learning how to add zest and flavor to your meals with healthy ingredients and spices and herbs is the name of the game. So go ahead and explore the many recipes in this book.

Playing Defense

Mother Nature protects plants from the environment and pests by giving them defenses, such as polyphenols and antioxidants. When we eat these plants, those defenses are transferred to us and help protect our health.

The table on the facing page lists a variety of "incredible ingredients" and their potential health benefits.

Don't Break Your Heart

Incredible Ingredient	Benefits	Tips
Avocados	Rich in heart healthy monounsaturated fat and potassium	Add avocados to your salads and sandwiches as your fat instead of cream and mayonnaise based dressings and spreads.
Beans, Peas, and Lentils	Another nutrient powerhouse, rich in minerals, fiber, and protein, for relatively low calories – the perfect partnership for keeping you satisfied until the next meal.	Add to all foods and eat at least ½ cup a day. Prepare with spices and herbs and do not add fat or meats. Also, dried lentils and peas only take 30 minutes to cook, unlike dried beans, so lose the cans and buy these dried.
Dark Chocolate (50 percent cocoa and above)	Rich in flavonoids, these foods take care of your cardiovascular system by taking care of the inside of your blood vessels to help blood flow smoothly to all organs and keeping your heart from having to work too hard.	Add cocoa powder to your favorite gravies, barbecue sauces, sauces, oatmeal, cereal, poultry and meat spices, and rubs. Add crunch to your fruit, yogurt, oatmeal, and salads with cocoa nibs.
Eggs	High quality protein and choline important for preventing build-up of homocysteine, and helps reduce chronic inflammation, both of which are associated with cardiovascular disease	Eat no more than one yolk a day to keep your cholesterol intake in check. The egg white does not contain any of the cholesterol, so feel free to add a few more egg whites, while limiting the yolks.
Fruits – fresh, frozen, dried	Rich in fiber, vitamins, minerals, and protective polyphenols and antioxidants. Great way to increase potassium intake for cardiovascular health	Make sure and get plenty of variety in your fruits. Try a different fruit every day. Also, try adding fruits to your cooking, meats, and salads.
Healthy Carbohydrates, Whole Grains, and Fiber (examples include brown rice, whole wheat pasta, fruits, and vegetables)	Highly satisfying to keep you feeling full longer. Rich in minerals and B vitamins with plenty of energy to keep you going. Whole grains and fiber are an important part of a heart healthy lifestyle by helping to decrease cholesterol and keep your vessels healthy. They can also help you meet your weight goals.	Pair with lean protein, such as poultry, fish, lean beef; as well as plenty of veggies for a complete meal.

Incredible Ingredient	Benefits	Tips
Healthy Fats	Great for taking care of your cardiovascular system. Monounsaturated and polyunsaturated fats are important for a heart healthy diet.	Choose foods rich in healthy fats such as raw nuts, avocados, olives, as well as olive, soy, and canola oils when cooking and for dressings.
Nuts	Nutrient powerhouses, rich in minerals, healthy fats, protein, and fiber. Just a handful fills you up.	High in fat and calories, keep this food to an ounce per serving. Add to your salads, casseroles, soups, meat rubs, sauces, and desserts
Oats	Low glycemic index, high in minerals, B vitamins, fiber, and energy	Oats are a great way to start your day, but can also be added to soups, sauces, meat and poultry rubs, and desserts.
Olives and Olive Oil	Rich in heart healthy monounsaturated fat	Add olives to your cooking and casseroles, as well as your favorite sandwiches and dips. When cooking always measure out your oil, as it is easy to add too much fat and calories, if not careful.
Peppers	Rich in phytochemicals and antioxidants, fiber, folate, minerals, vitamin B6, as well as one of the richest sources of vitamins C and A, including lutein, zeaxanthin, beta-carotene, and lycopene.	Eat a variety of hot and mild peppers to add rich nutrition and color to your meals…not to mention flavor and pizzazz.
Protein	Important for maintaining and building muscle to keep a strong metabolism and body. Lean protein is also highly satisfying and helps to keep you fuller longer.	Look for lean protein sources, such as poultry, fish, lean beef, low-fat and nonfat dairy, soy, beans, and lentils.
Red Wine and Purple Grape Juice	Rich in flavonoids and resveratrol, wine and grape juice help to take care of your cardiovascular system similar to cocoa and chocolate	Too much of a good thing can have the reverse effect on your heart. Keep intake to no more than 1 to 2 glasses (4 to 8 ounces) (115 to 225 g) a day.

Incredible Ingredient	Benefits	Tips
Soy	High quality protein plant food and heart healthy flavonoids.	Several choices from soybeans added to salads to tofu added to sauces, soups, and shakes. Include when you can for a protein and health boost.
Spices and Herbs	Rich in heart protecting antioxidants and polyphenols. Many also help to regulate blood sugar levels	Be creative and try adding different spices and herbs to your sauces, meats, salads, soups, and even your desserts and drinks.
Sweet Potatoes	One of the richest sources of vitamin A, also rich in antioxidants, and phytonutrients that decrease inflammation, with a low glycemic index.	Mash them, roast them, bake them, and eat them alone or add to your favorite casseroles and risotto. High versatility and great nutrient boost to any meal or dish.
Tea – green, white, black, and matcha (concentrated dried green tea leaves)	Rich in flavonoids, helps to take care of your cardiovascular system similar to cocoa and chocolate	Not just a beverage anymore, add tea to your sauces, dressings, poultry, and meat rubs.
Vegetables – including garlic and onions	Rich in fiber, vitamins, minerals, and protective phytochemicals and antioxidants; and low in calories. Great way to increase potassium intake for heart health.	Eat as many vegetables as you can. Get creative and add to as many meals and snacks as possible.

Pantry Makeover

Now that you know what ingredients to focus on, make sure your kitchen is stocked to support your heart-healthy diet. Toss out the salt and ready-made sauces and soups and add these ingredients to your kitchen to make your own fresh, flavorful, low-sodium dishes. Here is a list of foods to always have on hand.

Brown, red, and black rice
Easy and flavorful whole grains to add to your meals.

Cocoa and dark chocolate
Choose 50 percent cocoa and higher.

Dried peas, beans, and lentils

Edamame
These green soy beans can be found in the frozen food section.

Fruits and vegetables
Buy all colors and try fresh, frozen, and dried. Limit the dried to no more than about an ounce (25 g) since dried is concentrated in calories.

Garlic

Herbs and spices
Both dried and fresh. Keep a few fresh herb plants, like basil and thyme, on your windowsill.

Low-fat and nonfat dairy
Add Greek yogurt to soups and sauces for a protein boost.

Oats

Olive, soy, and canola oil

Onions

Peppers
Both hot and sweet

Raw nuts

Ready-to-eat greens
Good examples are kale, endive, baby spinach, and spring mix

Sweet potatoes

Tea
All kinds; choose loose so you can add to recipes.

Tofu
Add to shakes, soups, eggs, casseroles, and sauces for a nutrition boost.

Vinegar
All kinds; to make your own dressings and marinades.

Whole wheat bread and whole wheat pasta
Reduce the number of white, enriched grains.

chapter 3

Adding Flavor: Herbs and Spices

Low in sodium, spices and fresh and dried herbs add wonderful aroma and flavor to what otherwise could be bland, lackluster dishes. Just a pinch or two can easily transform a ho-hum meal into an exotic eating adventure.

Rich in potent antioxidants that help protect our cells from damage, spices and herbs are not only a smart alternative to sodium, they also have phytochemicals, such as flavonoids, phenolic acids, and volatile oils, all important for good health. Ancient civilizations such as the Maya used herbs as medicinal remedies and taught early explorers how to cook with them and use them in health tonics. With such a long history of healing, don't herbs and spices deserve a prominent spot in your cooking?

What is the difference between an herb and a spice?

Although people often use the terms interchangeably, herbs and spices are not the same. While both are parts of plants, the difference between the two is which part of the plant they originate from. Herbs come from the leafy and green part, while spices are parts from the root, stem, bulb, bark, or seeds. In fact, certain herbs and spices come from the same plant, just different parts. The leaves of the *Coriandrum sativum* plant, commonly known as coriander, give us cilantro, an herb, while its dried seeds give us coriander, a spice. And while herbs originated in and prefer the more temperate climates of Italy, France, and England, spices grow in more tropical countries. Since spices tend to be stronger in flavor, they are typically added in smaller amounts than their milder cousins.

Selecting, storing, and cooking with herbs

When selecting fresh herbs, look for consistent color, free from dark spots, wilting, and yellowing. Store herbs in loosely wrapped damp paper towels inside a closed plastic bag for no more than several days. Dried herbs should be kept in tightly sealed glass containers and placed in a cool and dark location. They maintain their flavor for about six months. Because most herbs are delicate they are best added towards the end of cooking to maintain their flavor and nutritional benefits.

Herb	Flavor	Uses
Basil	Several varieties – peppery to sweet, cinnamon, lemon, and Thai	Pesto, Thai, Vietnamese, and Italian dishes, soups, dips, salads, stews, sauces, tomato dishes
Bay leaf	Aromatic, pungent	Meats, sauces, soups, stews, vegetables
Chives	Sweet, oniony	Potatoes, eggs, cream soups, spreads
Dill weed	Pungent	Potatoes, fish, tomato soup, stewed lamb, sautéed spinach, yogurt sauces, rice pilaf
Marjoram	Sweet, similar to oregano	Soups, stews, marinades
Mint	Clean, fresh, cool, aromatic	Fruit salads, vegetables, soups, lamb
Oregano	Strong with bitter undertone, balsamic	Fish, meats, poultry, Italian and Greek dishes, sauces, soups, vegetables
Parsley	Peppery	Garnishes, sauces, soups, stews, eggs
Rosemary	Sweet	Fish, lamb, seafood, casseroles, salads, soups, vegetables
Sage	Slightly bitter, strong, spicy depending on specie	Fish, meats, poultry, salads, soups, stuffing, pizza
Savory	Peppery, similar to thyme	Soups, stews, beans, cabbage, meat, vegetables
Tarragon	Licorice, mint	Fish, chicken, vegetables, eggs
Thyme	Aromatic, pungent	Fish, meats, poultry, salads, stuffing, soups, tomato dishes, chowders
Turmeric	Earthy, pungent, bitter	Curries, Indian cuisine

Spice	Flavor	Uses
Allspice	Aromatic, similar to cloves, cinnamon, and nutmeg	Cakes and breads, sweet potatoes, vinaigrettes
Ancho chile pepper	Heat, sweet	Sauces, meat, sweets
Anise	Licorice	Baked goods, soups, pork
Black pepper	Heat, aromatic	Meat, chicken, vegetables
Cardamom	Citrus, spicy, floral	Baked goods, Indian cuisine, coffee
Cloves	Strong, pungent, sweet	Sweets, cider, wine, ham
Coriander	Lemon citrus	Pastries, cakes, vegetables, and vegetable and chicken soups
Cumin	Earthy	Meat stews, vegetables, couscous, meat, poultry, dips, marinades
Ginger	Earthy, pungent, citrus	Baked goods, fruits, vegetables, meat, fish
Nutmeg	Sweet, spicy	Baked goods, vegetables, custards, puddings
Paprika	Sweet, smoky, sometimes hot	Pork, chicken, chili, barbecue
Red pepper	Heat	Meat, seafood, salsa
Saffron	Earthy, pungent, slightly bitter	Bread, pastries, soups, rice
Vanilla	Warm, fruity, sweet, floral	Seafood, sauces, vegetables, confectionary, ice cream, soft drinks, puddings, cakes, cookies, liquors

The following recipes provide ways to incorporate herbs and spices into your cooking.
They are also featured in some of the recipes in this book.

Cocoa Tea Rub

Makes about 6 tablespoons (90 ml), enough for 1 pound (450 g) of poultry or meat

ingredients

2 tablespoons (30 ml) green tea leaves

2 tablespoons (30 ml) black tea leaves

2 tablespoons (30 ml) natural cocoa powder

¼ teaspoon (1 ml) ground cinnamon

steps

1. Mix all ingredients in a bowl.

2. Rub on poultry or meat prior to cooking.

Green Tea Rub

Makes about 6 tablespoons (90 ml), enough for 1 pound (450 g) of fish

ingredients

3 tablespoons (45 ml) dried green tea leaves

1 tablespoon (15 ml) onion powder

1 tablespoon (15 ml) dried basil

½ teaspoon (2 ml) ground cumin

steps

1. Mix all ingredients in a bowl.

2. Rub on fish prior to cooking.

Fruity Marinade

Makes 1 cup (250 ml)

ingredients

¼ cup (60 ml) fresh lime juice

¼ cup (60 ml) orange juice

¼ cup (60 ml) olive oil

1 tablespoon (15 ml) apple cider vinegar

2 teaspoons (10 ml) Dijon mustard

2 cloves garlic, minced

2 teaspoons (10 ml) ground cumin

2 teaspoons (10 ml) paprika

¼ teaspoon (1 ml) ground black pepper

steps

1. Whisk all ingredients in a bowl.

2. Use as a marinade for meats, poultry, or even as salad dressing.

Pomegranate Marinade

Makes 1 cup (250 ml)

ingredients

¼ cup (60 ml) cornstarch

1 cup (250 ml) pomegranate juice

¼ cup (60 ml) olive oil

1 garlic clove, minced

1 teaspoon (5 ml) fresh lime juice

1 teaspoon (5 ml) dried thyme

steps

1. Whisk cornstarch with 2 tablespoons (15 ml) cold water.

2. Add all ingredients to a saucepan.

3. Bring to a boil. Simmer until thickened.

4. Use as a marinade for meats, poultry, or even as salad dressing.

White Tea Glaze

Makes 2½ cups (375 ml)

ingredients

1 cup (250 ml) water

1½ cups (375 ml) packed brown sugar

1 tablespoon (15 ml) unsalted butter

1 tablespoon (15 ml) loose white tea in infuser or 1 bagged white tea

steps

1. Combine water, brown sugar, and butter in a saucepan. Add tea and remove once water begins to boil.

2. Boil for two minutes then simmer for 5 more minutes and let cool.

Herbed Yogurt Sauce

Makes 1 cup (250 ml)

ingredients

6 ounces (180 g) plain Greek yogurt

¼ cup (60 ml) fresh basil

¼ cup (60 ml) fresh mint

Juice of 1 lemon

1 clove garlic

1 teaspoon (5 ml) ground cumin

1 teaspoon (5 ml) ground coriander

Dash salt and pepper

1 cucumber, thinly sliced (optional)

steps

1. Place all ingredients in a food processor and pulse until combined.

2. Serve with grilled chicken or steak.

3. Garnish with thin slices of cucumber, if desired.

Thai Meat Marinade

Makes ½ cup (125 ml)

ingredients

4 tablespoons (60 ml) reduced-sodium soy sauce

2 tablespoons (30 ml) honey

2 tablespoons (30 ml) dark sesame oil

1 tablespoon (15 ml) minced fresh ginger

1 tablespoon (15 ml) minced garlic

½ teaspoon (2 ml) freshly ground black pepper

steps

Whisk ingredients together in a bowl until well blended.

Pecan Pesto

Makes ½ cup (125 ml)

ingredients

½ cup (125 ml) pecans

½ cup (125 ml) fresh parsley leaves

2 tablespoons (30 ml) fresh tarragon

1 clove garlic

¼ cup (60 ml) canola oil

¼ cup (60 ml) water

1 teaspoon (5 ml) fresh lemon juice

Dash salt and pepper

steps

1. Heat the oven to 350° F (175° C).

2. Spread pecans on a baking sheet and toast for 5 to 7 minutes.

3. Combine remaining ingredients in a food processor and purée. Add pecans and continue to blend until mixture is smooth. If mixture is too thick, add more water to thin to desired consistency.

4. Serve over whole wheat pasta, as a spread on whole wheat bread, or with poultry.

Gremolata Dressing

Makes 1 cup (250 ml)

ingredients

2 teaspoons (10 ml) grated lemon peel

¼ cup (60 ml) fresh lemon juice

2 tablespoons (30 ml) olive oil

2 tablespoons (30 ml) chopped fresh parsley

2 cloves garlic, minced

⅛ teaspoon (0.5 ml) freshly ground black pepper

steps

Whisk ingredients together until well blended.

Thai Dipping Sauce

Makes ¾ cup (175 ml)

ingredients

¼ cup (60 ml) corn syrup

3 tablespoons (45 ml) minced fresh
   cilantro

1 tablespoon (15 ml) fresh lime juice

¼ cup (60 ml) prepared Thai peanut sauce

steps

Whisk ingredients together until well blended.

Niçoise Dressing

Makes ¼ cup (60 ml)

ingredients

2 tablespoons (30 ml) extra-virgin olive oil

1 tablespoon (15 ml) Shiraz, or dry red wine

1 tablespoon (15 ml) red wine vinegar

2 teaspoons (10 ml) Dijon mustard

Freshly ground black pepper, to taste

steps

1. Whisk ingredients together until well blended.

2. Toss with salad greens.

Pineapple Salsa

Makes 6 cups (1,500 ml)

ingredients

1 (20-ounce) (20 g) can diced pineapple, or 3½ cups (875 ml) fresh

2 cups (500 ml) diced tomato

½ cup (125 ml) chopped fresh cilantro

3 jalapeno peppers, seeded and minced

2 cloves garlic, minced

Juice of 1 lime

steps

Combine ingredients until well blended.

Apricot Ginger Dressing

Makes 1¼ cups (310 ml)

ingredients

¾ cup (175 ml) fat-free ranch dressing

½ cup (125 ml) apricot preserves or jam

1 teaspoon (5 ml) Dijon style mustard

¾ teaspoon (4 ml) ground ginger

steps

1. Combine all ingredients.
2. Refrigerate until ready to use.

Cooking Tip: For a tropical topping, substitute mango chutney for the apricot preserves or jam.

Low-Fat Tartar Sauce

Makes ½ cup (125 ml)

ingredients

½ cup (125 ml) light mayonnaise

3 tablespoons (45 ml) sweet pickle relish

3 tablespoons (45 ml) dried onion

4 teaspoons (20 ml) Dijon mustard

2 teaspoons (10 ml) fresh lemon juice

steps

1. Combine all ingredients in a small bowl and mix well.
2. Refrigerate until ready to use.

Raspberry Vinaigrette

Makes 1 cup (250 ml)

ingredients

⅓ cup (75 ml) olive oil

¼ cup (60 ml) raspberry or red wine vinegar

2 tablespoons (30 ml) finely chopped shallots or red onion

2 tablespoons (30 ml) honey

2 tablespoons (30 ml) orange juice

steps

1. Whisk together all ingredients in a small bowl.

2. Refrigerate until ready to use. Mix again before serving.

Viva Mexico Salsa

Makes 2½ cups (625 ml)

ingredients

1 (15-ounce) (425-g) can fire-roasted crushed tomatoes

¼ cup (60 ml) corn kernels

¼ cup (60 ml) chopped yellow onions

2 tablespoons (30 ml) minced fresh cilantro

1 tablespoon (15 ml) fresh lime juice

1 teaspoon (5 ml) ground black pepper

½ teaspoon (2 ml) garlic powder

1 jalapeno pepper, finely chopped (optional)

steps

1. Combine all ingredients in a small bowl.

2. Refrigerate for at least 1 hour to allow flavors to blend.

Strawberry Balsamic Dressing

Makes 1 cup (250 ml)

ingredients

6 tablespoons (90 ml) extra-virgin olive oil

2 tablespoons (30 ml) balsamic vinegar

½ cup (125 ml) halved strawberries

¼ teaspoon (1 ml) salt

⅛ teaspoon (0.5 ml) freshly ground black pepper

1 teaspoon (5 ml) brown sugar

½ teaspoon (2 ml) roughly chopped fresh mint

steps

1. In the bowl of a food processor or blender, combine all ingredients. Blend until smooth.

2. Refrigerate until ready to use. Mix again before serving.

Guacamole

Makes 1½ cups (375 ml)

ingredients

1 ripe avocado, halved

1 medium tomato, chopped

¼ cup (60 ml) chopped yellow onion

1 tablespoon (15 ml) olive oil

1 teaspoon (5 ml) chopped fresh cilantro

1 teaspoon (5 ml) fresh lemon juice

steps

1. Using a spoon, scoop the avocado pulp from the shells and place in a bowl of a food processor or blender.

2. Add remaining ingredients and blend until smooth. Transfer to a serving dish.

chapter 4

Mighty Meats

Meaty Truths

Red meat, a rich source of nutrition, can be a part of a healthy diet.

Certain lean cuts of red meat are lower in saturated fat and cholesterol
than some kinds of fish and cuts of poultry.

Including a variety of sources of lean protein is important to a healthful diet.

More than half of the fat in lean red meat is the heart-healthy mono-unsaturated fat.

Featured Nutrients

Red meat is rich in protein, vitamin B12, B6, niacin, riboflavin, thiamin, iron,
zinc, phosphorus, magnesium, selenium, and potassium, as well as zinc,
cobalt, copper and selenium. All are important for overall health, especially
heart, muscle, brain, immune function, and energy production.
These nutrients work together to take care of our health.

Meat and the environment is a hot topic, as is any process that uses our natural resources. According to the Environmental Protection Agency, all agriculture accounts for 6 percent of greenhouse gases (GHG), with livestock production accounting for 2.8 percent. Interestingly, beef and pork rank lower than coffee, salad, fruit, and whole-grain cereal when measuring the embodied energy ratio (the total energy consumed during manufacturing, processing, and supplying a product). Adding to the confusion are the marketing and packaging terms used, such as grass-fed. It is perceived that grass-fed animals are more environmentally friendly, which, in fact, is incorrect. Grass-feeding uses more energy, more land, and more water than grain-feeding. Moreover, grass-fed animals produce more methane.

Red meat, which includes beef, pork, and lamb, can be a part of a heart-healthy diet. The key is moderation. Many studies show that red meat may increase risk of chronic illness; however, these studies include all cuts of meat, including processed meats. Healthy cuts of red meat are those that are low in fat, saturated fat, and cholesterol. Additionally, many of the processed meats have added preservatives and sodium, which negatively impacts health.

How to Choose Lean Meat

A rule of thumb for choosing leaner cuts of meat is to look for loin and round cuts.

FDA lean guidelines – in a 3.5 ounce serving, less than 10 g total fat, less than 4.5 g saturated fat, and less than 95 mg of cholesterol

Here is a list of cuts that satisfy the government's lean guidelines.

Bottom Round Roast
Bottom Round Steak
Sirloin Tip Center Steak
Sirloin Tip Side Steak
Tenderloin Roast
Tenderloin Steak
Top Loin Steak
Top Round Steak
Top Sirloin Steak

There are two basic cooking methods, moist heat and dry heat. As a rule of thumb, use moist heat for the less tender cuts, such as chuck, round, and rump to help break down connective tissue. Use dry heat for the more tender meats, such as those from the loin section. Tenderness is determined by the location on the animal, amount of fat marbling, age of animal (younger animals are more tender), meat storage, and preparation.

Cooking Tips for Beef

Tender Beef

- Salt meat after cooking to avoid drawing moisture out of meat during cooking.

- Handle ground meat as little as possible to avoid compacting beef granules into a tougher texture.

- Turn meat with tongs to avoid piercing with fork, which can release juices.

- If using a spatula, do not press down, as that squeezes out the juices.

Browning

Remove excess moisture from meat with paper towel before cooking as extra steam in pan can prevent browning.

Cutting Meat

Put meat in the freezer for about 30 minutes or until firm to make it easier to cut into strips or cubes.

Did You Know?

The loin section of the animal provides the most tender cuts. As you go farther from the loin the cuts of meat get less tender.

Meat continues to cook internally when removed from a heat source, so it is important to let meat "rest" to achieve desired doneness.

Cooking Methods

Method	Cut	How to...
Roasting – dry heat	Tender cuts	In oven, slow cooking at 325° F (160° C) until desired doneness is reached.
Broiling – dry heat	Tender cuts	In broiler pan in oven, 2 to 5 inches (5 to 12 cm) from heat. Broil one side until brown; season. Flip and repeat.
Pan-broiling – dry heat	Tender cuts	In pan, over direct heat. Do not add oil or water. Brown each side as meat cooks; drain fat as it accumulates.
Pan-frying – small amount oil	Tender cuts	Same as pan-broiling, except heat small amount of oil before adding meat.
Grilling – dry heat	Tender cuts	Use grill. Before heating grill seasoned meat at least 15 minutes prior to cooking; sear steak on each side, then reduce heat and cook to almost desired doneness. Let rest for 5 minutes to finish cooking.
		Rare: 120° to 125° F (52° to 51° C)
		Medium rare: 130° to 135° F (54° to 57° C)
		Medium: 140° to 145° F (60° to 63° C)
		Well done: your choice
Braising – moist heat	Less tender cuts	In pan, over direct heat, brown meat on all sides, drain fat, season, and add small amount of liquid. Cover tightly and finish cooking on top of range or in oven at 325° F (160° C).
Cooking in liquid – moist heat	Less tender cuts	In heavy pan, on top of range or in oven, brown meat, drain fat, season, and add enough liquid to cover meat. Cover pan tightly and simmer. Cook to desired doneness.

Honey Pork Tenderloin Kebobs

4 servings

ingredients

½ cup (125 ml) bourbon, or 2 tablespoons (30 ml) apple cider vinegar

½ cup (125 ml) honey

½ cup (125 ml) mustard

1 teaspoon (5 ml) dried tarragon

3 to 4 sweet potatoes, cut into 24 (1-inch) (2-cm) cubes

1½ pounds (680 g) pork tenderloin, cut into 24 (1-inch) (2-cm) cubes

4 medium ripe peaches, unpeeled, pitted, and quartered

4 green peppers, each cut into 8 (2-inch) (4-cm) pieces

8 yellow onions, each cut into 4 (2-inch) (4-cm) pieces

Olive oil, for grilling

Through changes in feeding and breeding techniques, pork is leaner than ever before. Today's pork has 16 percent less fat and 27 percent less saturated fat as compared to 1991. Many cuts of pork are now as lean as skinless chicken.

steps

1. Mix first four ingredients in a bowl; stir well and set glaze aside. Steam or boil sweet potatoes until crisp-tender.

2. Thread 3 sweet potato cubes, 3 pork cubes, 2 peach quarters, 4 green pepper pieces, and 4 onion pieces alternately onto each of 8 (10-inch) (25-cm) skewers.

3. Brush kabobs with honey-glaze mixture.

4. Lightly oil grill. Grill over medium-hot heat source 5 minutes on each side or until thoroughly heated, basting occasionally with glaze.

Nutrients per serving:

Calories: 501
Total Fat: 8 g
Saturated Fat: 4 g
Trans Fat: 0 g
Cholesterol: 105 mg
Sodium: 348 mg
Total Carbohydrates: 86 g
Dietary Fiber: 11 g
Sugars: 40 g
Protein: 21 g
Iron: 4 mg

Macronutrient Breakdown
69% Carbohydrates
17% Protein
14% Fat

Don't Break Your Heart

Tuscan Pork and Bean Salad

4 servings

Cuts with the words "loin" or "round" in their name, such as tenderloin, sirloin, eye of round, top round, are the leanest.

The traditional Mediterranean diet is considered one of the healthiest diets for heart health.

70% DV for vitamin C, and 60% DV for vitamin A

Nutrients per serving:

Calories: 338
Total Fat: 5 g
Saturated Fat: 1 g
Trans Fat: 0 g
Cholesterol: 84 mg
Sodium: 535 mg
Total Carbohydrates: 29 g
Dietary Fiber: 10 g
Sugars: 7 g
Protein: 45 g
Iron: 5 mg

Macronutrient Breakdown
34% Carbohydrates
53% Protein
13% Fat

ingredients

½ cup (125 ml) bourbon, or 2 tablespoons (30 ml) apple cider vinegar

½ cup (125 ml) honey

½ cup (125 ml) mustard

1 teaspoon (5 ml) dried tarragon

3 to 4 sweet potatoes, cut into 24 (1-inch) (2-cm) cubes

1½ pounds (680 g) pork tenderloin, cut into 24 (1-inch) (2-cm) cubes

4 medium ripe peaches, unpeeled, pitted, and quartered

4 green peppers, each cut into 8 (2-inch) (4-cm) pieces

8 yellow onions, each cut into 4 (2-inch) (4-cm) pieces

Olive oil, for grilling

4 tablespoons (20 ml) Parmesan cheese

steps

1. In a shallow serving bowl, toss together all ingredients, except for the Parmesan cheese.

2. Portion onto individual serving plates; top each serving with 1 tablespoon (5 ml) cheese.

Asian Grilled Pork Tenderloin with Pineapple

6 servings

Pineapple naturally contains bromelain, an enzyme that helps to decrease inflammation.

ingredients

2 lean pork tenderloins, each 12 to 16 ounces (350 to 450 g)

1 (6-ounce) (150-g) can pineapple juice

3 tablespoons (45 ml) reduced-sodium soy sauce

2 tablespoons (30 ml) minced fresh garlic

2 tablespoons (30 ml) minced fresh ginger

1 teaspoon (5 ml) ground cumin

1 teaspoon (5 ml) chili powder

½ teaspoon (2 ml) ground black pepper

2 cups (500 ml) fresh pineapple, peeled and cut into 1-inch (2.5-cm) cubes

steps

1. Place pork tenderloins in a resealable plastic bag; set aside. In a small bowl, combine marinade ingredients; pour over pork.

2. Seal bag; refrigerate for at least 1 hour to marinate, or up to 24 hours to enhance flavor.

3. Prepare medium-hot fire in a charcoal grill or preheat a gas grill to medium high. When ready to grill, remove pork from marinade and place on grill. Cook, covered, for about 10 minutes per side (about 20 minutes total) or until the internal temperature is 145° F (63° C), followed by a 3-minute rest time..

4. Meanwhile, thread the pineapple chunks onto 6 metal skewers; place on the grill during the last 6 minutes of grilling time, turning after 3 minutes.

5. To serve, slice pork into ½-inch (1-cm) slices (medallions) and serve with grilled pineapple.

Nutrients per serving:

Calories: 136
Total Fat: 2 g
Saturated Fat: 1 g
Trans Fat: 0 g
Cholesterol: 49 mg
Sodium: 316 mg
Total Carbohydrates: 13 g
Dietary Fiber: 1 g
Sugars: 8 g
Protein: 17 g
Iron: 1 mg

Macronutrient Breakdown
37% Carbohydrates
50% Protein
13% Fat

Thai Lettuce Wraps with Satay Pork

8 servings (appetizer)

ingredients

Vegetable oil cooking spray

4 boneless loin pork chops, each about 1-inch (2.5-cm) thick

Marinade

¼ cup (60 ml) reduced-sodium soy sauce

2 tablespoons (30 ml) honey

2 tablespoons (30 ml) dark sesame oil

1 tablespoon (15 ml) minced fresh ginger root

1 tablespoon (15 ml) minced garlic

½ teaspoon (2 ml) freshly ground black pepper

Wraps

3 large heads butter lettuce, leaves separated

2 medium carrots, peeled and cut into 2-inch (5-cm) matchsticks

1 English cucumber, cut into 2-inch (5-cm) matchsticks

2 ounces (57 g) bean thread (Asian cellophane noodles), soaked for 15 minutes in hot water and then drained

16 sprigs fresh cilantro

Sauce

¼ cup (60 ml) corn syrup

3 tablespoons (45 ml) minced fresh cilantro

1 tablespoon (15 ml) fresh lime juice

¼ cup (60 ml) prepared Thai peanut sauce

steps

1. Place chops in a large self-sealing plastic bag; combine marinade ingredients in a small bowl and pour over chops. Seal the bag and refrigerate 1 to 4 hours.

2. While pork marinates, arrange stack of large lettuce leaves attractively on a large serving platter. Place carrots, cucumber, bean thread, and cilantro leaves in small dishes and arrange on the serving platter.

3. In a small serving bowl or ramekin, mix together corn syrup, minced cilantro, and lime juice. Pour peanut sauce in small serving bowls or ramekins.

4. Remove pork from refrigerator 30 minutes prior to grilling. Prepare medium-hot fire in a charcoal grill or preheat a gas grill to medium high. Arrange the coals or burners so there is medium-low zone for finishing chops.

5. When ready to grill, remove chops from marinade and discard marinade. Spray the grill grate with vegetable oil spray. Grill pork directly over medium-high fire until seared, 3-4 minutes per side. Slide chops to cooler part of grill, cover, and continue to grill until pork registers 145° F (63° C) when checked with an instant-read thermometer, about 5 minutes longer. Transfer to a cutting board and let rest for 5 minutes before slicing.

6. Cut pork into thin slices. Lay 3 medium-sized leaves of lettuce on a serving platter and arrange pork on lettuce.

7. To assemble, place a lettuce leaf on an appetizer plate. Arrange 2 slices of pork on top of the lettuce. Mound a bit of carrot, cucumber, and bean thread over top. Add a couple cilantro leaves and drizzle sauce over top. Fold the lettuce to form a roll and enjoy.

Cooking Tip: Everything can be done ahead, even the pork. Marinate and grill the pork early in the day, or even the day before, and refrigerate the chops. Slice the pork just before serving. The sauces can be made and placed in serving bowls several hours ahead; the condiments can be assembled on the platter and then covered and refrigerated until ready to serve.

Nutrients per serving:

Calories: 251
Total Fat: 8 g
Saturated Fat: 2 g
Trans Fat: 0 g
Cholesterol: 29 mg
Sodium: 427 mg
Total Carbohydrates: 32 g
Dietary Fiber: 2 g
Sugars: 11 g
Protein: 14 g
Iron: 2 mg

Macronutrient Breakdown
51% Carbohydrates
21% Protein
28% Fat

Peachy Mustard Pork Chop

4 servings

ingredients

¼ cup (60 ml) peach preserves

⅓ cup (75 ml) honey mustard

2 tablespoons (30 ml) fresh lemon juice

4 boneless loin pork chops, each ¾-inch (2-cm) thick

1 red onion, thinly sliced and grilled (optional)

Cherry tomatoes, for garnish (optional)

1 ripe peach, sliced (optional)

steps

1. Stir together preserves, mustard, and lemon juice.

2. Prepare medium-hot fire in a charcoal grill or preheat a gas grill to medium high. Grill chops, turning occasionally and basting with sauce just until done, 8 to 9 minutes, or until internal temperature on a thermometer reads 145° F (63° C), followed by a 3-minute rest time. Discard any leftover basting sauce.

3. Garnish with grilled red onion, tomatoes and peach. Serve with Spicy Brussels Sprouts (see page 53).

Lemon juice is the strongest food acid in the kitchen. Disinfect your cutting board by wiping the surface with a lemon slice.

Nutrients per serving:

Calories: 294
Total Fat: 11 g
Saturated Fat: 4 g
Trans Fat: 0 g
Cholesterol: 81 mg
Sodium: 197 mg
Total Carbohydrates: 18 g
Dietary Fiber: 1 g
Sugars: 14 g
Protein: 33 g
Iron: 1 mg

Macronutrient Breakdown
23% Carbohydrates
44% Protein
33% Fat

Don't Break Your Heart

Spicy Brussels Sprouts

4 servings

ingredients

¾ teaspoon (4 ml) olive oil

4 cups (500 ml) Brussels sprouts, ends trimmed, halved

⅓ cup (75 ml) low-sodium tomato sauce

steps

1. Place olive oil in a sauté pan set over medium-high heat.

2. Add brussels sprouts to the pan and cook 5 to 7 minutes until they start to soften.

3. Add tomato sauce and pepper flakes and cook 3 to 4 more minutes. Remove from heat and serve.

Nutrients per serving:

Calories: 294
Total Fat: 11 g
Saturated Fat: 4 g
Trans Fat: 0 g
Cholesterol: 81 mg
Sodium: 197 mg
Total Carbohydrates: 18 g
Dietary Fiber: 1 g
Sugars: 14 g
Protein: 33 g
Iron: 1 mg

Macronutrient Breakdown
23% Carbohydrates
44% Protein
33% Fat

Curry Beef and Fruit and Almond Basmati Rice

4 servings

ingredients

1 pound (450 g) boneless beef top sirloin steak

2 tablespoons (30 ml) reduced-sodium soy sauce

2 teaspoons (10 ml) minced garlic

1 cup (250 ml) non-flavored almond milk

1 to 2 teaspoons (5 to 10 ml) Thai red curry paste

Fruit and Almond Basmati Rice (see recipe on page 55)

1 teaspoon (5 ml) vegetable oil

1 cup (250 ml) fresh green beans, trimmed

¼ cup (60 ml) chopped fresh basil

1 teaspoon (5 ml) minced lemon grass

Basil leaves, for garnish (optional)

Curry is native to India, Pakistan, Sri Lanka, and South East Asia.

In Thailand, curry is a stew-like dish made with coconut milk, curry paste, and meat.

Red curry paste is typically made with dried red chilies, cilantro root, coriander, cumin, garlic, shallots, kaffir lime rind, lemongrass, shrimp paste, sea salt, and galangal, a member of the ginger family but with a very different taste.

steps

1. Cut beef steak lengthwise in half, then crosswise into ¼-inch (0.5-cm) strips. Combine soy sauce and garlic in a medium bowl. Add beef and toss. Set aside.

2. Whisk almond milk and curry paste in a small bowl until well blended; set aside.

3. Prepare Fruit and Almond Basmati Rice according to the directions on page 55.

4. While rice is cooking, heat oil in a large nonstick skillet set over medium-high heat until hot. Add ½ of beef and stir-fry 1 to 2 minutes or until outside of beef is no longer pink. Remove from the skillet. Repeat with remaining beef. Remove from the skillet and keep warm.

5. In the same skillet, bring almond milk mixture to a boil. Reduce heat; simmer 5 minutes, stirring occasionally. Add green beans, basil, and lemon grass; bring to a boil. Reduce heat and simmer 11 to 13 minutes, or until green beans are crisp-tender, stirring occasionally.

6. Return beef with juice to the skillet: cook, stirring, until heated through. Serve over rice. Garnish with basil, if desired.

Nutrients per serving:

Calories: 338
Total Fat: 5 g
Saturated Fat: 1 g
Trans Fat: 0 g
Cholesterol: 84 mg
Sodium: 535 mg
Total Carbohydrates: 29 g
Dietary Fiber: 10 g
Sugars: 7 g, Protein: 45 g
Iron: 5 mg

Macronutrient Breakdown
34% Carbohydrates
53% Protein
13% Fat

Fruit and Almond Basmati Rice

4 servings

ingredients

1 cup (250 ml) basmati rice

¾ cup (175 ml) chopped mixed dried fruit

¼ cup (60 ml) slivered almonds, toasted

steps

Prepare rice according to package directions, omitting butter
or oil. Add dried fruit and toasted almonds during stand time.

Nutrients per serving:

Calories: 494
Total Fat: 11 g
Saturated Fat: 2 g
Trans Fat: 0 g
Cholesterol: 68 mg
Sodium: 483 mg
Total Carbohydrates: 67 g
Dietary Fiber: 6 g
Sugars: 18 g
Protein: 33 g
Iron: 5 mg

Macronutrient Breakdown
53% Carbohydrates
27% Protein
20% Fat

Sirloin with Sugar Snap Peas and Pasta Salad

4 servings

ingredients

2 cups (500 ml) fresh sugar snap peas

2 cups (500 ml) cooked corkscrew pasta

1 cup (250 ml) grape tomatoes, halved

½ cup (125 ml) Gremolata Dressing, divided (see page 31)

3 cloves garlic, minced

1 teaspoon (5 ml) ground black pepper

1 pound (450 g) boneless beef top sirloin

Freshly grated lemon peel (optional)

Chopped fresh parsley (optional)

Beef is a major source of iron. It would take 3 cups (750 ml) of spinach to get the same amount of iron in 3 ounces (90 g) of beef.

Gremolata, a chopped herb condiment made of lemon zest, parsley, and garlic, is a popular condiment in Milan.

steps

1. Bring water to a boil in a large saucepan. Add sugar snap peas; cook 2 to 3 minutes until crisp-tender. Drain and rinse under cold water. Combine sugar snap peas, pasta, and tomatoes in a large bowl. Set aside.

2. Toss 2 tablespoons (30 ml) Gremolta Dressing with pasta mixture. Set aside.

3. Combine 3 cloves minced garlic and 1 teaspoon black pepper; press evenly onto beef steak. Place steak on rack in a broiler pan so surface of beef is 2 to 3 inches (5 to 7.5 cm) from heat. Broil 9 to 12 minutes for medium rare, turning once.

4. Carve steak into thin slices. Add steak slices and remaining dressing to pasta mixture; toss to coat evenly. Garnish with grated lemon peel and parsley, if desired.

Nutrients per serving:

Calories: 331
Total Fat: 12 g
Saturated Fat: 2.7 g
Trans Fat: 0 g
Cholesterol: 68 mg
Sodium: 77 mg
Total Carbohydrates: 25 g
Dietary Fiber: 3 g
Sugars: 4 g
Protein: 30 g
Iron: 4 mg

Macronutrient Breakdown
31% Carbohydrates
36% Protein
33% Fat

Beef, Mango, and Barley Salad

6 to 8 servings

ingredients

1 (1½- to 2-pound) (675- to 900-g) lean beef sirloin tri-tip roast

2 medium red bell peppers, cut into bite-size pieces

1½ (7 ml) teaspoons sweet paprika

1 cup (250 ml) uncooked quick-cooking barley

¼ teaspoon (1 ml) ground black pepper

⅓ cup (75 ml) fresh lime juice

1 teaspoon (5 ml) olive oil

2 medium mangoes, cut into bite-size pieces

⅓ cup (75 ml) chopped green onions

¼ cup (60 ml) chopped fresh cilantro

4 large Boston lettuce leaves

Mango trees, first recorded in Asia around 2000 BC, were not introduced to U.S. soil until the 1860s.

Mango adds an interesting punch to this salad, both with its sweetness and with a boost of vitamin C and vitamin A.

steps

1. Preheat the oven to 425° F (220° C). Place bell peppers on a metal baking sheet; spray with nonstick cooking spray. Set aside.

2. Press 1 teaspoon (5 ml) paprika evenly onto all surfaces of beef roast. Place roast on a rack in a shallow roasting pan. Do not add water or cover. Roast for 30 to 40 minutes for medium rare or 40 to 45 minutes for medium. Roast bell peppers in oven with beef for about 30 minutes or until tender. Set peppers aside to cool.

3. Remove roast when an instant-read thermometer registers 135° F (57° C) for medium rare or 150° F (65° C) for medium. Transfer roast to a carving board; tent loosely with aluminum foil. Let stand 15 minutes.

4. Meanwhile, cook barley according to package directions. Set aside to cool slightly.

5. Cut beef into ½-inch (1-cm) pieces; season with black pepper. Whisk lime juice, oil, and ½ teaspoon (2 ml) paprika in a small bowl until blended. Toss with beef, barley, roasted peppers, mangoes, green onions, and cilantro in a large bowl. Serve in Boston lettuce leaves.

Cooking Tip: To quickly cool barley and prevent it from clumping, spread the grains on a metal baking sheet.

Nutrients per serving:

Calories: 456
Total Fat: 14 g
Saturated Fat: 4 g
Trans Fat: 0 g
Cholesterol: 83 mg
Sodium: 63 mg
Total Carbohydrates: 55 g
Dietary Fiber: 8 g
Sugars: 21 g
Protein: 32 g
Iron: 4 mg

Macronutrient Breakdown
47% Carbohydrates
27% Protein
26% Fat

30-Minute Beef Goulash

4 servings

ingredients

10 ounces (284 g) fully cooked lean beef pot roast with gravy

2 tablespoons (30 ml) olive oil

2 large portobello mushrooms, chopped

1 medium onion, chopped

1 pound (450 g) red-skinned potatoes, diced and boiled until tender

1 (14-ounce) (397-g) can reduced-sodium beef broth

1 teaspoon (5 ml) paprika

½ teaspoon (2 ml) ground black pepper

Goulash, a soup or stew made with beef, paprika, onion, and root vegetables, originated in Hungary in the 19th century.

steps

1. Cut pot roast into bite-size pieces.

2. Heat oil in a small Dutch oven set over medium heat until hot. Add mushrooms and onion; cook, stirring, for 5 minutes.

3. Add beef, gravy, and potatoes to the Dutch oven; stir in broth, paprika, and pepper. Bring to a boil. Reduce heat to medium; cook 10 minutes, or until goulash is heated through and slightly thickened, stirring occasionally.

Cooking Tip: Eight ounces (225 g) baby Portobello mushrooms, cut into quarters, or 1 cup (250 ml) chopped white mushrooms can be substituted for large Portobello mushrooms.

Nutrients per serving:

Calories: 316
Total Fat: 12 g
Saturated Fat: 3 g
Trans Fat: 0 g
Cholesterol: 71 mg
Sodium: 235 mg
Total Carbohydrates: 22 g
Dietary Fiber: 2 g
Sugars: 3 g
Protein: 28 g,
Iron: 3 mg

Macronutrient Breakdown
30% Carbohydrates
36% Protein
34% Fat

Lamb Niçoise

4 servings

ingredients

Lamb

2 lamb eyes of loin

1 tablespoon (15 ml) olive oil

¾ pound (340 g) green beans, lightly blanched and refreshed in chilled water

12 fingerling potatoes, halved and boiled until tender

⅓ cup (75 ml) black olives

2 hard-cooked eggs, quartered

Dressing

2 tablespoons (30 ml) extra-virgin olive oil

1 tablespoon (15 ml) Shiraz, or dry red wine

1 tablespoon (15 ml) red wine vinegar

2 teaspoons (10 ml) Dijon mustard

Freshly ground black pepper, to taste

steps

1. Remove sinew from lamb. Heat oil in a nonstick pan set over medium heat. Sauté lamb for 2 to 3 minutes on each side for medium rare. Cover with foil and allow to rest 5 to 10 minutes. Lamb can also be chilled to serve as a cold salad.

2. Place beans, potatoes, and olives in a bowl.

3. Whisk all dressing ingredients together; season with pepper to taste. Reserve 1 tablespoon (15 ml). Gently toss through the salad.

4. To serve, slice lamb across the grain. Arrange vegetables and eggs on a serving platter or individual plates. Top with lamb and drizzle with the reserved dressing.

Lamb is a significant source of omega-3s and monounsaturated fats, healthy fats that contribute to cardiovascular health.

Niçoise (pronounced knee-SWAHZ) is a French word meaning, "in style of Nice" – for Nice, France.

Nutrients per serving:

Calories: 680
Total Fat: 22 g
Saturated Fat: 5 g
Trans Fat: 0 g
Cholesterol: 183 mg
Sodium: 322 mg
Total Carbohydrates: 85 g
Dietary Fiber: 10 g
Sugars: 8 g
Protein: 36 g
Iron: 8 mg

Macronutrient Breakdown
50% Carbohydrates
21% Protein
29% Fat

Lamb Kabobs Wrapped in Pita

4 to 6 servings

ingredients

1½ pounds (680 g) boneless leg of lamb, cut into 1-inch (2.5-cm) cubes

1 tablespoon (15 ml) plus 1 teaspoon (5 ml) fresh chopped thyme

2 cloves minced garlic, divided

½ teaspoon (2 ml) freshly ground black pepper

1 cup (250 ml) plain whole-milk yogurt

1 tablespoon (15 ml) fresh lemon juice

4 to 6 large whole wheat pitas

Chopped lettuce (optional)

Diced tomato (optional)

Lean and tender lamb is great for grilling, broiling, and roasting.

Lamb is meat from a 4-month to 1-year-old sheep, while mutton is meat from a sheep over 1 year old.

81% daily needs for protein and 47% DV for zinc

steps

1. Place lamb in a large bowl. Combine 1 tablespoon (15 ml) of the thyme, half the garlic, and pepper; add to lamb and toss well. Cover and leave for 20 minutes to allow the flavors to infuse. Thread onto metal or presoaked wooden skewers.

2. Place yogurt in a small bowl and add remaining thyme and garlic and lemon juice. Mix well. Season to taste with salt and pepper.

3. Broil or barbecue the kabobs over medium to high heat until cooked as desired, about 4 to 5 minutes each side for medium rare.

4. Toast pitas lightly on the grill until just warmed, and top with lettuce and tomato, if desired. Remove lamb from the skewers and place on salad. Drizzle with yogurt and wrap firmly into a roll.

Cooking Tip: The lamb can be diced and seasoned the day before and stored, covered, in the refrigerator. Allow to stand at room temperature for 5 to 10 minutes before cooking. The yogurt mixture can also be made a day ahead and refrigerated in a sealed container.

Nutrients per serving:

Calories: 424
Total Fat: 12 g
Saturated Fat: 4 g
Trans Fat: 0 g
Cholesterol: 105 mg
Sodium: 449 mg
Total Carbohydrates: 39 g
Dietary Fiber: 5 g
Sugars: 3 g
Protein: 41 g
Iron: 5 mg

Macronutrient Breakdown
37% Carbohydrates
38% Protein
25% Fat

Don't Break Your Heart

Honey-Dijon Veal and Zucchini Stir-Fry

4 servings

ingredients

4 ounces (115 g) uncooked spaghetti

1 pound (450 g) veal leg cutlets

3 teaspoons (15 ml) olive oil

1 medium onion, cut into thin wedges

1 medium zucchini, cut lengthwise in half, then cut crosswise into thin slices

¼ cup (60 ml) nonfat honey-Dijon salad dressing

1 tablespoon (15 ml) water

Veal is lighter in color than beef because of the young age of the calf and lower iron level in the meat.

54% of total fat is heart-healthy monounsaturated fat.

steps

1. Cook spaghetti according to package directions; keep warm.

2. Meanwhile, if necessary, pound veal cutlets to ⅛-inch (0.3-cm) thickness. Stack cutlets; cut into 3- x 1-inch (7.5- x 2.5-cm) strips.

3. In a large nonstick skillet set over medium-high, heat 1 teaspoon (5 ml) oil until hot. Add ½ of veal and stir-fry 1 to 2 minutes or until outside surface is no longer pink. (Do not overcook.) Remove veal from the skillet. Repeat with remaining veal and another 1 teaspoon (5 ml) oil.

4. In the same skillet, heat remaining 1 teaspoon (5 ml) over medium-high heat until hot; stir-fry onion for 2 minutes. Add zucchini; stir-fry for 3 minutes, or until crisp-tender. Add salad dressing and water. Return veal to skillet; toss to combine. Heat through and serve over spaghetti.

Nutrients per serving:

Calories: 313
Total Fat: 6 g
Saturated Fat: 1 g
Trans Fat: 0 g
Cholesterol: 88 mg
Sodium: 328 mg
Total Carbohydrates: 35 g
Dietary Fiber: 2 g
Sugars: 7 g
Protein: 29 g
Iron: 2 mg

Macronutrient Breakdown
46% Carbohydrates
37% Protein
17% Fat

Savory Veal Stew

8 servings

ingredients

2½ pounds (2 kg) veal for stew, cut into 1-inch (2.5-cm) pieces

⅓ cup (75 ml) all-purpose flour

½ teaspoon (2 ml) ground black pepper

3 tablespoons (45 ml) olive oil

1 large onion, coarsely chopped

3 large cloves garlic, minced

1 (14-ounce) (397-g) can reduced-sodium chicken broth

2 teaspoons (10 ml) dried thyme

1 pound (450 g) baby carrots

1 pound (450 g) small new red-skinned potatoes, halved

1 cup (250 ml) frozen peas

On average, a trimmed, cooked 3-ounce (90-g) serving of veal contains 166 calories and only 5.6 grams of fat. Because of veal's low fat content, it has very little waste and 1 pound (450 g) of veal can yield four 3-ounce (90-g) servings.

steps

1. Combine flour and pepper. Lightly coat veal with flour mixture. Heat oil in a Dutch oven set over medium heat until hot. Brown veal in batches; remove from the Dutch oven.

2. Add onion and garlic to the Dutch oven; cook and stir for 1 minute. Add veal, broth, and thyme; bring to a boil. Reduce heat; cover tightly and simmer for 45 minutes.

3. Add carrots and potatoes; continue cooking, covered, for 30 minutes, or until veal and vegetables are fork-tender. Skim fat. Stir in peas; heat through.

Nutrients per serving:

Calories: 410
Total Fat: 12 g
Saturated Fat: 3 g
Trans Fat: 0 g
Cholesterol: 205 mg
Sodium: 322 mg
Total Carbohydrates: 21 g
Dietary Fiber: 4 g
Sugars: 5 g
Protein: 53 g
Iron: 4 mg

Macronutrient Breakdown
22% Carbohydrates
52% Protein
26% Fat

Don't Break Your Heart

chapter 5

Fantastic Fish

Fins of Truth

U.S. Dietary Guidelines and the American Heart Association recommend 2 servings of fish—about 8 ounces (225 g) per week—for better cardiovascular health.

Use healthful cooking methods such as baking, broiling, and grilling to lower fat and calories.

Choose wild fish more often and eat a variety to reduce your exposure to contaminants.

Featured Nutrients

Red meat is rich in protein, vitamin B12, B6, niacin, riboflavin, thiamin, iron, zinc, phosphorus, magnesium, selenium, and potassium, as well as zinc, cobalt, copper and selenium. All are important for overall health, especially heart, muscle, brain, immune function, and energy production. These nutrients work together to take care of our health.

Farm-Raised Versus Wild

Which is healthier—farmed fish or wild? The answer depends on the type of fish. Certain types of fish are perfectly safe and only available from fish farms, while others may come either farmed or wild. Studies suggest that certain farm-raised fish in the United States, such as a few types of salmon, may be contaminated with harmful chemicals like PCBs, dioxins, and mercury. Keep in mind, though, that according to many experts, the benefits of eating fish outweigh any health risks associated with these potential toxins. Your best bet is to eat a variety of fish, which can reduce your exposure to any particular contaminant.

The Environmental Impact

Concern that eating fish may have a detrimental impact on the environment deters some people from eating fish. Knowing the facts can help consumers make healthful decisions to include this wonderful lean protein source as part of a healthful diet. Additionally, fisheries are taking steps to improve their methods, such as adding messages to package labels.

Overfishing and the unintended capture of bycatch is a worldwide problem. The Food and Agriculture Organization of the United Nations reports that new, economical methods are being put into practice, such as new types of fishing devices that allow unwanted bycatch to escape safely. Additionally, according to the U.S. National Oceanic and Atmospheric Administration, the United States is making headway in rebuilding overfished populations and has rebuilt 21 stocks since the year 2000. Many of the overfished stocks include the typical menu fare, such as red snapper, Chinook and Coho salmon, bluefin tuna, grouper, Atlantic cod, and Atlantic halibut. However, you don't need to cut out fish altogether to make a difference. Instead, make *greener* choices by selecting fish from lists by several responsible organizations.

Why Eating Fish Is Good for You

Fish is rich in omega-3s, a type of unsaturated fat that promotes blood flow through the heart and vessels. People who eat fish tend to have a lower risk of heart disease, heart attacks, and stroke. In addition, omega-3s help keep the brain healthy, so fish eaters tend to have lower rates of depression and cognitive decline associated with aging. DHA (docosahexaenoic acid) and EPA (eicosapentaenoic acid) have been shown to promote brain growth and development for fetuses and babies. Eating fish, then, is as important for pregnant women as for other adults. And as a rich source of lean protein, with less saturated fat than most meat or poultry, fish can help with weight loss and maintenance, a good tactic for keeping the heart healthy.

According to the Monterey Bay Aquarium Seafood Watch, the best choices for the environment and human health are albacore tuna, freshwater Coho salmon, wild-caught Alaskan salmon, wild-caught Pacific sardines, farmed rainbow trout, Dungeness crab, farmed mussels, farmed Arctic char, and farmed oysters. By choosing these particular fish you can help the environment and put your mind at ease. Plus, they are a great addition to a heart-healthy diet.

The American Heart Association and the U.S. Dietary Guidelines recommend consuming 2 servings or 8 ounces (225 g) of fish per week.

Fish Richest in Omega-3s

Seafood (3 ounces) (25 g)	EPA milligrams	DHA milligrams	Total long-chain omega-3s
Anchovies	649	99	748
Canned tuna, white	198	535	733
Herring	1056	751	1807
Mackerel	369	677	1046
Mussels	235	430	665
Oysters	372	212	584
Salmon, farm-raised	587	1238	1825
Salmon, wild	349	1215	1564
Sardines	402	433	835
Trout	220	575	795

source: National Fisheries Institute

Omega-3s in Most Popular Fish

Seafood (3 ounces) (25 g)	EPA milligrams	DHA milligrams	Total long-chain omega-3s
Canned tuna			
Light	40	190	230
White	198	535	733
Catfish	42	109	151
Clams	117	124	241
Cod	3	131	134
Crab	207	196	403
Flatfish	207	219	426
Pollock	77	383	460
Salmon:			
Farm-raised	587	1238	1825
Wild	349	1215	1564
Shrimp	145	122	267
Tilapia	4	111	115

source: National Fisheries Institute

Fish Cooking Tips
(adapted from the National Fisheries Institute)

How to Know When Fish Is Fully Cooked

Whole fish, larger fillets, or steaks

Use an instant-read thermometer; when the temperature approaches 140° F (60° C) remove from the heat source to prevent overcooking. Let fish rest 2 to 3 minutes before serving.

Thinner fillets

Use an instant-read thermometer; when the temperature approaches 140° F (60° C) remove from the heat source to prevent overcooking. Let the fish rest 2 to 3 minutes before serving.

Shellfish

Mussels or clams are cooked after 3 to 5 minutes and the shells open. Once most of the shellfish have opened, discard any that remain closed.

Shrimp and scallops are cooked after 2 to 3 minutes per side. They appear opaque and their texture is slightly firm. Shrimp turn orange or pink.

Lobsters and crabs take anywhere from 5 to 25 minutes to cook. The shells turn a deep red and the meat changes from translucent to opaque. Use an instant-read thermometer for large pieces of meat, such as lobster tails. When the temperature reaches 140° F (60° C), the lobster is cooked.

Cooking Methods
(adapted from the National Fisheries Institute)

Method	How to	Good for...
Steaming	A gentle, fat-free cooking method that keeps the natural moisture in foods. Steam from a simmering liquid, such as wine, water, or broth, to cook the fish. Include ingredients such as lemon juice, white wine, onions, shallots, spices, or fresh herbs in the cooking liquid to add subtle, delicious flavor.	Delicate seafood to protect against drying
Grilling	Spray both sides of fish with olive oil or vegetable oil to prevent sticking. Add flavor by marinating the seafood in juice, herbs, spices, and oils. Seafood steaks and whole fish will take about 10 minutes to cook for each inch (cm) of thickness (measured in depth, not length). Thin fillets will take less time.	Meatier, firmer-fleshed finfish cut into steaks or fillets with skin. Flakier finfish, skinless fillets, and smaller shellfish can be grilled using a grill basket.
Microwaving	Cover food with microwave-safe plastic wrap or place in a microwave-safe, covered casserole dish to lock in steam. Moisten the fish with a small amount of seasoned liquid or broth, but do not submerge it completely.	Thin, skinless fillets of fish
Poaching	Submerge fish in a bath of flavorful liquid that's kept just below the boiling point (160° to 180° F) (70° to 80° C).	Whole fillets of sturdy finfish, such as salmon
Broiling	Spray fish with oil and season with salt and pepper or submerge it in a quick marinade and shake off any excess. Place it skin side down (if there is skin) on a lightly oiled, heat-proof broiling pan or cookie sheet and cook under the heating source until almost cooked through. Finfish will just begin to flake and the color will turn from translucent to almost opaque; shrimp and scallops will feel firm, not mushy, when poked with tongs, and the flesh will have just turned opaque; lobster tails will turn a bright, rosy color and the flesh will turn from translucent to opaque.	Fillets or steaks of finfish, large scallops or shrimp, and lobster tails. For thin fillets and small pieces of seafood, move the rack so that it is only about 2 inches (5 cm) from the heat source. For larger pieces of seafood, move the broiling rack 4 to 6 inches (10 to 15 cm) away from the heat source so that the inside cooks before the outside dries out or becomes tough.
Pan Searing	Heat a low-sided, well-seasoned skillet on the stovetop over medium-high heat with a teaspoon of oil and swirl the pan to evenly coat it; heat until almost smoking. Add the seafood. Turn the seafood once it is about halfway cooked through. Fish will appear opaque on the side closest to the bottom of the pan and translucent on the side that is facing up. Continue cooking on the second side until the fish reaches a final cooking temperature of 140° F (60° C), or the meat just begins to flake and becomes opaque.	Fish steaks and thicker, shorter fillets of fish
Baking	To roast a whole fish, preheat the oven to about 450° F (230° C). Make a few vertical slashes on each side of a cleaned fish. (This will help ensure even cooking and flavors). Place the fish on a rimmed cookie sheet or shallow pan to catch any juices that escape. As the fish roasts, baste it with the juices that accumulate in the bottom of the pan until the flesh at its thickest point just begins to flake and turns from translucent to opaque. Estimate that it will take about 8 to 10 minutes per inch of thickness for the fish to cook through. Rotate the pan about half way through cooking time to cook evenly.	Whole fish. (Smaller, delicate pieces of fish do not respond as well to baking and require a coating of bread crumbs or a splash of broth or olive oil to keep them moist.)

Savory Fish Fillets

4 servings

ingredients

1 pint cherry tomatoes, halved

¼ cup (60 ml) pitted ripe olives, halved

1 tablespoon (15 ml) chopped parsley

1 tablespoon (15 ml) red wine vinegar

4 (4-ounce) (113-g) cod fillets

3 tablespoons (45 ml) Dijon mustard, divided

1 (15-ounce) (425 g) can low-sodium chicken broth

1 clove garlic, pressed

1 cup (250 ml) quick-cooking brown rice

1 zucchini, sliced in rounds

steps

1. Combine the first 4 ingredients in a small bowl, stir well, and set aside.

2. Pat fillets dry with paper towels. Spread 1 tablespoon (15 ml) mustard over fillets; set aside.

3. Combine broth, remaining 2 tablespoons (30 ml) mustard, and garlic in a large saucepan.

4. Add rice and stir. Cover, reduce heat, and simmer for 2 to 3 minutes. Stir in zucchini.

5. Arrange fillets on top of rice mixture; cover and simmer for about 8 minutes, or until liquid is absorbed and fish flakes easily with a fork. Spoon tomato mixture over top of fish before serving.

For most species, truly fresh fish is almost odorless. Fish begin to smell when deterioration sets in. This is often caused by incorrect storage practices that bring about the release of oxidized fats and acids through bacterial and enzymatic action.

Nutrients per serving:

Calories: 216
Total Fat: 3 g
Saturated Fat: 0 g
Trans Fat: 0 g
Cholesterol: 50 mg
Sodium: 441 mg
Total Carbohydrates: 22 g
Dietary Fiber: 3 g
Sugars: 4 g
Protein: 25 g
Iron: 2 mg

Macronutrient Breakdown
41% Carbohydrates
46% Protein
13% Fat

Seafood Orzo Risotto

4 servings

ingredients

1 tablespoon (15 ml) olive oil

½ cup (125 ml) finely chopped onion

1 clove garlic, minced

1 cup (250 ml) uncooked whole wheat orzo

2 cups (500 ml) low-sodium chicken broth

1 cup (250 ml) skim milk

½ cup (125 ml) diced zucchini

½ pound (225 g) raw medium shrimp, peeled, deveined, and halved lengthwise

½ pound (225 g) scallops, quartered if large

½ cup (125 ml) frozen peas, thawed

¼ cup (60 ml) minced fresh parsley

3 tablespoons (45 ml) grated Parmesan cheese

Shrimp range in size from about ½ inch (1 cm) long to almost 1 foot (30 cm).

In one spawning, shrimp produce about 500,000 eggs.

steps

1. Heat oil in a large, heavy nonstick skillet set on medium heat. Sauté onion and garlic until soft.

2. Add orzo, broth, and milk and bring to boil. Turn heat to low and simmer for about 10 minutes. Stir in zucchini, shrimp, scallops, and peas.

3. Simmer, stirring, for about 10 minutes, until liquid is absorbed. Cover and simmer for 5 minutes more until seafood is opaque.

4. Stir in parsley and Parmesan cheese and serve.

Nutrients per serving:

Calories: 307
Total Fat: 6 g
Saturated Fat: 2 g
Trans Fat: 0 g
Cholesterol: 91 g
Sodium: 301 mg
Total Carbohydrates: 34 g
Dietary Fiber: 4 g
Sugars: 6g
Protein: 29g
Iron: 3 mg

Macronutrient Breakdown
44% Carbohydrates
38% Protein
18% Fat

Halibut with a Heart

6 servings

ingredients

Steaks

2 pounds (900 g) halibut steaks, or haddock, grouper, or red snapper fillets

⅓ teaspoon (1.5 ml) salt

⅓ teaspoon (1.5 ml) ground black pepper

2 tablespoons (30 ml) light trans-free margarine, melted

Sauce

2 tablespoons (30 ml) light trans-free margarine

1 cup (250 ml) minced onion

1 cup (250 ml) grape tomatoes, halved

⅓ teaspoon (1.5 ml) red pepper flakes

½ teaspoon (2 ml) salt

steps

1. To cook steaks, preheat the broiler. Sprinkle steaks with salt and pepper; brush with margarine. Broil for 5 to 8 minutes or until fish is firm and opaque.

2. To make sauce, melt margarine in a saucepan; add onion and cook just until tender, about 5 minutes.

3. Add remaining ingredients and simmer, stirring occasionally, for 10 minutes.

4. Place halibut steaks on a serving platter and spoon the sauce over them.

The National Oceanic and Atmospheric Administration estimates the average American eats about one serving of seafood a week, approximately 3.5 ounces (100 ml).

The U.S. Food and Drug Administration (FDA) estimates pregnant women eat less than half a serving per week.

Nutrients per serving:

Calories: 236
Total Fat: 7 g
Saturated Fat: 1 g
Trans Fat: 0 g
Cholesterol: 48 mg
Sodium: 468 mg
Total Carbohydrates: 8 g
Dietary Fiber: 2 g
Sugars: 5 g
Protein: 33 g
Iron: 2 mg

Macronutrient Breakdown
25% Carbohydrates
62% Protein
13% Fat

Whole Wheat Crusted Tilapia

4 servings

ingredients

4 (4-ounce) (115-g) tilapia fillets

1 lemon

1 tablespoon (15 ml) olive oil

1 clove garlic, minced

Lemon pepper, to taste

½ cup (125 ml) unseasoned whole wheat bread crumbs

Most fish contain very little natural salt and can be included in a low-sodium diet.

steps

1. Preheat the oven to 450° F (230° C).

2. Spray a baking sheet with nonstick cooking spray. Place fish on baking sheet.

3. Squeeze lemon into a small bowl. Add olive oil and garlic and combine. Drizzle mixture over fillets. Season fillets with lemon pepper.

4. Sprinkle bread crumbs over fish. Bake until fish flakes easily when tested with a fork, about 8 to 10 minutes.

*To make your own whole wheat bread crumbs, cut the crusts off 2 to 3 slices of whole wheat bread and bake at 250° F (120° C), or toast until crusty; pulse in food processor until crumbs form.

Nutrients per serving:

Calories: 178
Total Fat: 6 g
Saturated Fat: 1 g
Trans Fat: 0 g
Cholesterol: 48 mg
Sodium: 84 mg
Total Carbohydrates: 7 g
Dietary Fiber: 1 g
Sugars: 1 g
Protein: 24 g
Iron: 1 mg

Macronutrient Breakdown
16% Carbohydrates
54% Protein
30% Fat

Honey-Broiled Sea Scallops

4 servings

ingredients

3 tablespoons (45 ml) fresh lime juice

1 tablespoon (15 ml) canola oil

1 tablespoon (15 ml) honey

1 teaspoon (5 ml) low-sodium soy sauce

¼ teaspoon (1 ml) ground ginger

1 pound (450 g) large sea scallops

2 tablespoons (30 ml) sesame seeds

Sea scallops are large, usually about 1½ inches (3.8 cm) in diameter, while bay scallops average about ½ inch (1 cm) in diameter.

steps

1. Combine lime juice, oil, honey, soy sauce, and ginger in a bowl. Add scallops and toss to coat. Cover and refrigerate for 1 hour, stirring occasionally.

2. Remove scallops from marinade, reserving marinade. Thread scallops evenly on 4 skewers. Place the skewers on a shallow baking pan that has been sprayed with nonstick cooking oil.

3. Broil 4 to 6 inches from heat source for 2 to 3 minutes. Turn and baste with reserved marinade and continue cooking for 2 to 3 minutes or until opaque throughout.

4. Place sesame seeds on wax paper and roll each skewer over seeds to evenly coat scallops. Serve immediately.

Nutrients per serving:

Calories: 176
Total Fat: 7 g
Saturated Fat: 1 g
Trans Fat: 0 g
Cholesterol: 37 mg
Sodium: 228 mg
Total Carbohydrates: 9 g
Dietary Fiber: 1 g
Sugars: 5 g
Protein: 20 g
Iron: 1 mg

Macronutrient Breakdown
19% Carbohydrates
45% Protein
36% Fat

Grilled Salmon with Avocado Tarragon Sauce

4 servings

ingredients

1 ripe avocado, pitted and peeled

⅓ cup (75 ml) nonfat plain or Greek yogurt

2 tablespoons (30 ml) fresh lemon juice

3 tablespoons (45 ml) extra-virgin olive oil, divided

1 sprig fresh tarragon

1 small clove garlic

½ teaspoon (2 ml) kosher salt

Freshly ground black pepper

4 (6-ounce) (170-g) skinless salmon fillets

1 teaspoon (5 ml) honey

There are seven species commonly referred to as Pacific salmon: Chinook, chum, Coho, pink, sockeye, masu, and amago. Atlantic salmon is a species within the genus Salmo.

Salmon is one of the best sources of heart-healthy omega-3 fats.

Omega-3s keep the blood flowing through vessels, making them healthy for the heart as well as the brain.

steps

1. Place avocado, yogurt, lemon juice, 2 tablespoons olive oil, tarragon, garlic, salt, and a few turns of pepper in a food processor and process until smooth. Set aside.

2. Preheat the grill to high and lightly oil the grate.

3. Combine remaining tablespoon of olive oil and honey and brush on both sides of salmon. Sprinkle with salt and pepper.

4. Place the salmon on the prepared grill and cook until easily flaked with a fork, 4 to 5 minutes per side.

5. Top each fillet with a dollop of avocado sauce.

Nutrients per serving:

Calories: 332
Total Fat: 22 g
Saturated Fat: 3 g
Trans Fat: 0 g
Cholesterol: 60 g
Sodium: 349 mg
Total Carbohydrates: 10 g
Dietary Fiber: 3 g
Sugars: 6g
Protein: 23 g
Iron: 1 mg

Macronutrient Breakdown
12% Carbohydrates
28% Protein
60% Fat

Festive Thai Shrimp

4 servings

ingredients

8 ounces (225 g) uncooked whole wheat linguine

1 tablespoon (15 ml) canola oil

1 small onion, thinly sliced

1 cup baby tomatoes, halved

8 ounces (225 g) mushrooms, sliced

4 ounces (115 g) asparagus

1½ cups (375 ml) low-sodium chicken broth

3 tablespoons (45 ml) all-purpose flour

¼ cup (60 ml) prepared Thai peanut sauce or peanut satay stir-fry sauce

1 pound (450 g) small or medium cooked fresh shrimp, or frozen, thawed

1/4 cup (60 ml) coarsely chopped dry roasted peanuts

steps

1. Cook linguine according to package directions. Drain and set aside.

2. While linguine is cooking, heat oil in a large saucepan or Dutch oven set over medium-high heat. Add onion and sauté for 2 minutes, stirring frequently. Add mushrooms and asparagus and cook an additional 2 minutes.

3. In a small bowl, whisk together broth, flour, and peanut sauce until well blended.

4. Add broth mixture to vegetables and bring to a simmer, stirring constantly.

5. Reduce the heat and continue to simmer, stirring gently, until the mixture thickens, about 2 minutes.

6. Add linguine and shrimp and heat through.

7. Place in individual bowls, top with peanuts, and serve.

Nutrients per serving:

Calories: 484
Total Fat: 13 g
Saturated Fat: 2 g
Trans Fat: 0 g
Cholesterol: 136 g
Sodium: 374 mg
Total Carbohydrates: 57 g
Dietary Fiber: 9 g
Sugars: 8 g
Protein: 35 g
Iron: 6 mg

Macronutrient Breakdown
47% Carbohydrates
29% Protein
24% Fat

Grilled Trout Tacos with Pineapple Salsa

12 servings

ingredients

1¾ cups (425 ml) julienned jicama

1½ cups (375 ml) thinly sliced red onion

1 cup fresh lime juice

12 (4-ounce) (115-g) rainbow trout fillets

24 (6-inch) (15-cm) whole wheat tortillas

1 head romaine lettuce, shredded

1 red bell pepper, sliced

Pineapple salsa (see recipe on page 32)

steps

1. Combine jicama, onion, and lime juice; let stand for 30 minutes.

2. Grill or sauté trout fillets until just done, about 2 minutes per side. Remove skin and break trout into bite-size pieces.

3. Toss trout with jicama mixture.

4. Meanwhile, on a very hot griddle, heat tortillas in batches.

5. Fill each tortilla with ¼ cup (60 ml) lettuce, red pepper slices, and ½ cup (125 ml) trout mixture. Serve with pineapple salsa on the side.

Trout has nearly 50 percent of the omega-3s of salmon, making it a good source of the healthy fat.

A high intake of vitamin B12 has been shown to be protective against colon cancer.

Nutrients per serving:

Calories: 341
Total Fat: 9 g
Saturated Fat: 2 g
Trans Fat: 0 g
Cholesterol: 66 mg
Sodium: 89 mg
Total Carbohydrates: 38 g
Dietary Fiber: 6 g
Sugars: 10 g
Protein: 28 g
Iron: 3 mg

Macronutrient Breakdown
43% Carbohydrates
33% Protein
24% Fat

Change-of-Pace Tuna Casserole

6 servings

ingredients

1 (10-ounce) (283.5-g) can condensed 98 percent fat-free,
reduced-sodium cream of mushroom soup

½ cup (125 ml) light sour cream

½ pound (225 g) whole wheat rotini pasta, cooked according to
package directions

2 tablespoons (30 ml) chopped pimiento

2 tablespoons (30 ml) trans-free margarine

½ pound (225 g) fresh mushrooms, sliced

½ cup (125 ml) chopped onion

½ cup (125 ml) chopped celery

2 (6-ounce) (170-g) cans of tuna, drained

½ cup (125 ml) sliced almonds, toasted

Studies have shown that eating seafood at least twice a week reduces the risk of heart disease by 30 to 40 percent.

Omega-3s in fish have been found to lower triglycerides, reduce inflammation, reduce blood pressure, and slow the buildup of plaque in arteries — all protective to cardiovascular health.

steps

1. Preheat the oven to 350° F (180° C).

2. In a bowl, blend soup with sour cream until smooth. Add pasta and
    pimiento; set aside.

3. Melt margarine in a sauté pan and sauté mushrooms, onions, and
    celery until vegetables are tender, about 5 minutes.

4. Mix vegetables into soup mixture; fold in tuna.

5. Pour tuna mixture into a lightly-greased 1½-quart baking dish.
    Top with almonds. Bake, uncovered, about 25 minutes or until
    hot and bubbly.

Cooking Tip: To make this meal more nutritious, add a 10-ounce
(283.5-g) package of thawed, frozen vegetables, such as chopped broccoli
or mixed stir-fry vegetables, when you add the pasta to the soup in step 2.

Nutrients per serving:

Calories: 335
Total Fat: 11 g
Saturated Fat: 3 g
Trans Fat: 0 g
Cholesterol: 31 mg
Sodium: 416 mg
Total Carbohydrates: 37 g
Dietary Fiber: 7 g
Sugars: 5 g
Protein: 22 g
Iron: 3 mg

Macronutrient Breakdown
44% Carbohydrates
26% Protein
30% Fat

Light Crab Dip

8 servings

ingredients

1 (8-ounce) (225-g) package nonfat cream cheese

½ cup (125 ml) light sour cream or plain low-fat yogurt

2 tablespoons (30 ml) light mayonnaise

1 tablespoon (15 ml) fresh lemon juice

1¼ teaspoons (6 ml) Worcestershire sauce

½ teaspoon (2 ml) dry mustard

Pinch onion salt

1 cup (250 ml) crabmeat

Few drops milk, for consistency

Reduced-fat cheddar cheese, grated, for topping

2 tablespoons (30 ml) chopped green onions

steps

1. In an ovenproof dish, combine cream cheese, sour cream or yogurt, mayonnaise, lemon juice, Worcestershire sauce, mustard, and onion salt. Fold in crabmeat.

2. Add few drops of milk to make creamy.

3. Stir in cheese to taste and sprinkle more over top.

4. Bake at 325° F (160° C) for 30 minutes. Garnish with chopped green onions and serve with toasted crusty bread.

Nutrients per serving:

Calories: 72
Total Fat: 2 g
Saturated Fat: 1 g
Trans Fat: 0 g
Cholesterol: 35 mg
Sodium: 312 mg
Total Carbohydrates: 4 g
Dietary Fiber: 0 g
Sugars: 2 g
Protein: 9 g
Iron: 0 mg

Macronutrient Breakdown
25% Carbohydrates
50% Protein
25% Fat

Don't Break Your Heart

Dijon Salmon

4 servings

ingredients

1 pound (450 g) salmon fillet

1 tablespoon (15 ml) Dijon mustard

2 tablespoons (30 ml) honey

Omega-3s are good for the brain as well as the heart. Intake of omega-3s and omega-3 containing fish has been found to improve mood and decrease risk of depression and cognitive decline in older persons.

steps

1. Preheat the oven to 425° F (220° C). Rinse salmon fillet and place on a baking sheet coated with nonstick spray.

2. Mix mustard and honey and brush over salmon.

3. Bake 10 to 20 minutes, depending on thickness of fillet, until salmon is mostly cooked through. Let rest for 5 minutes. Serve with Rosemary Potatoes (see page 91).

Nutrients per serving:

Calories: 143
Total Fat: 6 g
Saturated Fat: 1 g
Trans Fat: 0 g
Cholesterol: 40 mg
Sodium: 121 mg
Total Carbohydrates: 9 g
Dietary Fiber: 0 g
Sugars: 9 g
Protein: 14 g
Iron: 0 mg

Macronutrient Breakdown
23% Carbohydrates
39% Protein
38% Fat

Rosemary Potatoes

4 servings

ingredients

2 pounds (900 g) small red potatoes

1 tablespoon (15 ml) olive oil

2 tablespoons (30 ml) fresh rosemary, or 2 teaspoons dried

1 teaspoon (5 ml) garlic powder

steps

1. Preheat the oven to 400° F (200° C). Line a baking sheet with foil; set aside.

2. Scrub potatoes and quarter.

3. Place potatoes in a resealable plastic bag bag with olive oil and shake. Pour onto the prepared sheet.

4. Sprinkle with rosemary and garlic powder.

5. Bake 30 minutes, or until potatoes are soft and easily pierced with a fork.

Nutrients per serving:

Calories: 212
Total Fat: 4 g
Saturated Fat: 1 g
Trans Fat: 0 g
Cholesterol: 0 mg
Sodium: 46 mg
Total Carbohydrates: 39 g
Dietary Fiber: 5 g
Sugars: 4 g
Protein: 5 g
Iron: 2 mg

Macronutrient Breakdown
74% Carbohydrates
9% Protein
17% Fat

Baked Fish Sticks

8 servings

ingredients

Canola oil spray

1 cup (250 ml) whole wheat bread crumbs*

1 cup (250 ml) high-fiber bran cereal

1 teaspoon (5 ml) lemon pepper

½ teaspoon (2 ml) garlic powder

½ teaspoon (2 ml) paprika

½ cup (125 ml) whole wheat flour

2 large egg whites, beaten

2 pounds (900 g) tilapia fillets, cut into strips

Tilapia have become a favorite fish in the United States. Farmed tilapia have very low levels of mercury, making them a smart choice.

steps

1. Preheat the oven to 450° F (230° C). Set a wire rack on a baking sheet; coat with cooking spray.

2. Place bread crumbs, cereal flakes, lemon pepper, garlic powder, and paprika in a food processor and process until ground. Transfer to a shallow dish.

3. Place flour in a second dish and egg whites in a third dish.

4. Dredge each strip of fish in the flour, dip in the egg, then coat with the bread crumb mixture. Place on the prepared rack. Spray both sides of fish with cooking spray.

5. Bake until the fish is cooked through and breading is golden brown and crisp, about 10 minutes. Serve with low-fat tartar sauce (see recipe on page 33).

*To make your own whole wheat bread crumbs, cut the crusts off 3 to 4 slices of whole wheat bread and bake at 250° F (120° C), or toast until crusty; pulse in a food processor until crumbs form.

Nutrients per serving:

Calories: 193
Total Fat: 3 g
Saturated Fat: 1 g
Trans Fat: 0 g
Cholesterol: 48 mg
Sodium: 160 mg
Total Carbohydrates: 17 g
Dietary Fiber: 3 g
Sugars: 1 g
Protein: 25 g,
Iron: 3 mg

Macronutrient Breakdown
34% Carbohydrates
52% Protein
14% Fat

Don't Break Your Heart

White Wine Mussels

2 servings

ingredients

2 pounds (900 g) fresh mussels

1 cup (250 ml) dry white wine

2 cloves garlic, minced

1 onion, chopped

1 tomato, chopped

¼ cup (60 ml) fresh parsley, chopped

steps

1. Rinse mussels under cold water; remove beards. Discard any that have opened or have cracked shells.

2. Place mussels in a large pot and top with wine, garlic, and onion.

3. Cover the pot and set on high heat.

4. Cook 6 to 8 minutes, shaking pot, until mussels open.

5. Remove mussels with a slotted spoon to a serving dish. Place tomatoes in pot for 1 to 2 minutes.

6. Pour broth over mussels and sprinkle with parsley. Serve with crusty whole-grain bread, if desired.

Nutrients per serving:

Calories: 166
Total Fat: 2 g
Saturated Fat: 1 g
Trans Fat: 0 g
Cholesterol: 27 mg
Sodium: 187 mg
Total Carbohydrates: 14 g
Dietary Fiber: 2 g
Sugars: 8 g
Protein: 23 g
Iron: 4 mg

Macronutrient Breakdown
34% Carbohydrates
55% Protein
11% Fat

"Fried" Calamari

4 servings

ingredients

¼ cup (60 ml) whole wheat bread crumbs*

½ teaspoon (2 ml) dried oregano

½ teaspoon (2 ml) dried basil

½ teaspoon (2 ml) dried parsley

¼ cup (60 ml) whole wheat flour

1 egg white, beaten

1 pound cleaned squid, cut into

½-inch (1-cm) rings

steps

1. Preheat the oven to 425° F (220° C). Spray a cooking sheet with nonstick spray.

2. Mix bread crumbs and herbs.

3. Place flour, egg white, and bread crumb mixture in 3 different bowls.

4. A few at a time, dredge rings in flour, dip in egg, and coat with bread crumb mix.

5. Place on the prepared sheet and bake 8 to 10 minutes until cooked through.

*To make your own whole wheat bread crumbs, cut the crusts off 3 to 4 slices of whole wheat bread and bake at 250° F (120° C) or toast until crusty; pulse in food processor until crumbs form.

Nutrients per serving:

Calories: 167
Total Fat: 2 g
Saturated Fat: 1 g
Trans Fat: 0 g
Cholesterol: 302 mg
Sodium: 70 mg
Total Carbohydrates: 14 g
Dietary Fiber: 2 g
Sugars: 0 g
Protein: 23 g
Iron: 2 mg

Macronutrient Breakdown
34% Carbohydrates
55% Protein
11% Fat

chapter 6

Powerful Poultry

Poultry Clucks of Truth

For a lean, high protein food, choose the white meat portion of poultry without the skin.

Chicken skin is about 50 percent fat by weight.

Federal law does not permit the use of hormones in the production of poultry.

Poultry is the best food source of vitamin B6, which helps the body utilize energy from carbohydrates and protein, strengthens the immune system, creates red blood cells, and produces neurotransmitters, important for brain function.

Featured Nutrients

The following nutrients in poultry help build strong muscles and bones, boost the immune system, and aid in thyroid function:

Protein, B vitamins, niacin and B6, phosphorus, and selenium

Versatile Poultry

Poultry encompasses the ubiquitous chicken and turkey, as well as specialty birds, such as domestic duck, ostrich, emu, and squab. These birds add great variety to our meals. Packed with protein and no carbohydrates, they pair wonderfully with starchy and non-starchy vegetables and whole grains. Their mild flavor and versatility in preparation makes them perfect when using heart-healthy herbs and spices to add flavor and pizzazz.

Cooking Poultry

For a tender, juicy meal, cook poultry slowly with even heat. Young poultry, which is more tender, should be cooked with dry heat methods, while older, less tender birds are best cooked with moist heat methods. Many recommend brushing chicken with butter or margarine prior to cooking. If you must add fat to your bird, limit the amount to no more than 1 tablespoon (15 ml) of heart-healthy olive oil. All poultry should be cooked to an internal temperature of 165° F (75° C) to kill any bacteria.

Tip: Cooking bags are a convenient and easy way to cook a tender and juicy bird. And, as a bonus, vegetables can be added to the bag.

Cooking Methods

Method	Where	How to...
Broiling	In the oven, in pan, set oven to broil	Place bird skin side down on rack in pan; keep about 5 to 10 inches from heat source; after 30 minutes season, turn chicken, and broil another 20 minutes.
Roasting	In the oven, in pan, set oven to 325° F (160° C)	Place bird breast side up in a shallow pan; tent with foil; baste to brown the skin; remove foil about 20 minutes prior to completed roasting.
Grilling	On grill rack, over medium heat	Place bone side up; turn once halfway through grilling; cook to internal temperature of 165° F (75° C) and immediately remove. Approximate cooking times: Whole chicken: 40 to 50 minutes Thick pieces: 35 minutes Half a breast, tenderloin: 12 to 15 minutes
Pan-broiling	In pan, over medium heat	Do not add oil or water; brown each side as meat slowly cooks; drain fat as it accumulates.
Pan-frying	In pan, over high heat	Same as pan-broiling, except heat small amount of oil and add meat.
Braising	In pan, over medium heat	Brown meat on all sides; drain fat; season and add small amount of liquid; cover tightly; finish cooking on top of range or in oven at 325° F (160° C).
Cooking in liquid	In heavy pan, on top of range or in oven	Brown meat; drain fat; season and add enough liquid to cover meat; cover pan tightly; simmer. Cook to desired doneness.

Chicken with Golden Raisins, Green Olives, and Lemon

8 servings

ingredients

2 tablespoons (30 ml) olive oil

2 chickens, cut into pieces

½ teaspoon (2 ml) ground black pepper

2 cloves garlic, minced

1 teaspoon (5 ml) turmeric

1 teaspoon (5 ml) grated ginger

1 (2-inch) stick cinnamon

2 lemons, 1 juiced and 1 sliced

1 cup (250 ml) low-sodium chicken broth

2 potatoes, peeled and cut into ½-inch (1-cm) slices

4 carrots, peeled and thinly sliced

1 cup (250 ml) golden raisins

½ cup (125 ml) pimento-stuffed Spanish olives

Olive trees are first harvested after 15 years of growth.

The oldest olive tree is more than 2,000 years old. Most live for 300 to 600 years.

steps

1. Preheat the oven to 400° F (200° C).

2. In a large nonstick pan or Dutch oven, warm oil over medium-high heat. Sprinkle chicken with pepper. Add chicken pieces to the pan and brown on all sides, turning at least once. Remove chicken from the pan and set aside.

3. Lower heat to medium. Add garlic, turmeric, ginger, and cinnamon stick to the pan; cook, stirring constantly, for 15 seconds.

4. Pour lemon juice and broth into the pan, stirring to scrape up browned bits. Return chicken to the pan.

5. Place potatoes, carrots, raisins, olives, and lemon slices around the chicken. Raise heat to high and bring to a boil.

6. Cover the pan and place in the oven for 45 minutes. Remove the lid and continue to cook for another 10 minutes, or until cooked through. Serve immediately.

Nutrients per serving:

Calories: 387
Total Fat: 9 g
Saturated Fat: 2 g
Trans Fat: 0 g
Cholesterol: 99 mg
Sodium: 333 mg
Total Carbohydrates: 36 g
Dietary Fiber: 4 g
Sugars: 17 g
Protein: 42 g
Iron: 2 mg

Macronutrient Breakdown
37% Carbohydrates
43% Protein
20% Fat

Don't Break Your Heart

Grilled Chicken Pesto and Arugula Sandwich

4 servings

ingredients

¼ cup (60 ml) olive oil

2 tablespoons (30 ml) fresh lemon juice

1 clove garlic, minced

½ teaspoon (2 ml) freshly ground black pepper

1 pound (450 g) chicken cutlets

1 whole wheat baguette, cut into

4 equal pieces

¼ cup (60 ml) basil pesto*

1 large tomato, cut into 8 slices

1 cup (250 ml) packed baby arugula

Pesto, a sauce made from basil, garlic, nuts, and cheese, originated in Northern Italy.

Pesto comes from the Italian word, pesta, *which means "to pound or crush."*

steps

1. To make the marinade, combine olive oil, lemon juice, garlic, and pepper and pour into a resealable plastic bag. Add chicken and marinate for at least 30 minutes. Remove chicken from bag and reserve marinade.

2. Heat the grill on high. Add chicken, grill for 2 to 3 minutes, turn, and grill for another 2 to 3 minutes, or until chicken registers 165° F (74° C) on an instant read thermometer. Remove chicken from the grill and reserve.

3. Spread pesto on one half of each baguette. Add grilled chicken, arugula, and 2 tomato slices. Top each sandwich with the other half of the baguette. Add grilled chicken, arugula, and 2 tomato slices.

4. Brush the outside of each sandwich with about 1 teaspoon (5 ml) of leftover marinade.

5. Place on grill, reduce heat to medium, and grill for 2 to 3 minutes per side, or until bread is nicely toasted with grill marks.

6. Remove from heat and serve.

*See Pecan Pesto recipe on page 30 or use store-bought.

Nutrients per serving:

Calories: 356
Total Fat: 15 g
Saturated Fat: 3 g
Trans Fat: 0 g
Cholesterol: 44 mg
Sodium: 489 mg
Total Carbohydrates: 27 g
Dietary Fiber: 10 g
Sugars: 2 g
Protein: 24 g
Iron: 2 mg

Macronutrient Breakdown
30% Carbohydrates
29% Protein
41% Fat

Savory Chicken Primavera

6 servings

ingredients

Marinade

1 tablespoon (15 ml) balsamic vinegar

1 tablespoon (15 ml) red wine vinegar

Juice from ½ lemon

2 teaspoons (10 ml) ground black pepper

2 teaspoons (10 ml) ground ginger

1½ teaspoons (7 ml) paprika

6 boneless, skinless chicken breasts, cubed

1 small onion

2 red bell peppers

2 broccoli crowns

2 zucchini

4 tomatoes

2 cups (500 ml) spinach

1 tablespoon (15 ml) olive oil

4 cloves garlic, minced

1 cup (250 ml) low-sodium chicken broth

¼ cup (60 ml) picante sauce

6 ounces (170 g) feta cheese

24 ounces (680 g) cooked whole wheat pasta

Primavera *means "spring" in Italian.*

Created by a New York City chef in the 1970s, pasta primavera is an Italian-American dish containing pasta and fresh vegetables.

steps

1. Combine marinade ingredients and pour into a resealable plastic bag. Dice chicken breasts and add to marinade. Marinade chicken for at least 30 minutes.

2. Roughly chop onion, bell peppers, broccoli, zucchini, tomatoes, and spinach.

3. Warm olive oil in a large, heavy saucepot set over medium heat. Sauté garlic for 1 to 2 minutes. Add onions, broccoli, peppers, and zucchini. Cook until onions are just starting to soften. Add chicken and marinade and cook, stirring occasionally, for about 5 minutes.

4. Add spinach, chicken broth, picante sauce, and chopped tomatoes. Cover and let stew, stirring occasionally.

5. When chicken is almost cooked through, add feta cheese and simmer until feta is melted.

6. Serve chicken primavera sauce over whole wheat pasta.

Nutrients per serving:

Calories: 487
Total Fat: 9 g
Saturated Fat: 3 g
Trans Fat: 0 g
Cholesterol: 75 mg
Sodium: 600 mg
Total Carbohydrates: 60 g
Dietary Fiber: 11 g
Sugars: 9 g
Protein: 43 g
Iron: 4 mg

Macronutrient Breakdown
49% Carbohydrates
35% Protein
16% Fat

Don't Break Your Heart

Alamo Chicken

4 servings

ingredients

3 avocados

1 large onion, diced

20 grape tomatoes, halved

1 (15-ounce) (425-g) can no-salt-added corn

1 (6-ounce) (170-g) can sliced black olives, drained

3 ounces Italian dressing

2 tablespoons (30 ml) garlic powder

4 boneless, skinless chicken breasts

Low-fat sour cream and paprika, for topping (optional)

Built in 1718, the Alamo, a former mission and fortress compound in San Antonio, Texas, is where the Battle of the Alamo was fought in 1836.

steps

1. Peel and dice avocado. Combine diced avocado, onion, and tomatoes in a bowl. Add corn and black olives.

2. Mix together Italian dressing and garlic powder and pour over mixture. Stir to combine. Refrigerate until ready to serve.

3. Heat the grill on high. Add chicken, grill for 2 to 3 minutes, turn, and grill for another 2 to 3 minutes, or until chicken registers 160° F (70° C) on an instant read thermometer.

4. Serve at once with the avocado-corn mixture.

5. Top with sour cream and paprika, if desired.

Nutrients per serving:

Calories: 450
Total Fat: 22 g
Saturated Fat: 3 g
Trans Fat: 0 g
Cholesterol: 66 mg
Sodium: 406 mg
Total Carbohydrates: 35 g
Dietary Fiber: 13 g
Sugars: 14 g
Protein: 32 g
Iron: 3 mg

Macronutrient Breakdown
30% Carbohydrates
28% Protein
42% Fat

Chicken and Tortilla Olé

4 servings

ingredients

1 (10-ounce) (283.5-g) can condensed low-sodium cream of chicken soup

½ cup (125 ml) fat-free plain Greek yogurt

4 ounces low-fat Cheddar cheese

½ teaspoon (2 ml) dried rosemary

1 tablespoon (15 ml) wheat germ

4 boneless, skinless chicken breasts

1 (10-ounce) (283.5-g) package frozen mixed vegetables, thawed

8 (6-inch) (15-cm) corn tortillas

¼ cup (60 ml) sliced black olives (optional)

Olé, a Spanish expression used to denote excitement and approval, is commonly used at bullfights.

steps

1. Preheat the oven to 350° F (175° C).

2. In an ovenproof casserole dish, combine soup, yogurt, cheese, rosemary, and wheat germ. Add chicken breasts and vegetables to mixture.

3. Place corn tortillas on top and bake for 35 minutes, or until internal temperature reaches 165° F (75° C).

4. Top with olives if desired and serve.

Nutrients per serving:

Calories: 476
Total Fat: 8 g
Saturated Fat: 3 g
Trans Fat: 0 g
Cholesterol: 112 mg
Sodium: 590mg
Total Carbohydrates: 43 g
Dietary Fiber: 6 g
Sugars: 5 g
Protein: 58 g
Iron: 3 mg

Macronutrient Breakdown
37% Carbohydrates
48% Protein
15% Fat

Stuffed Chicken Breasts with Herbed Ricotta

4 servings

ingredients

4 ounces (115 g) low-fat ricotta

1 tablespoon (15 ml) each minced tarragon, basil, parsley, and chives

2 tablespoons (30 ml) olive oil, divided

4 boneless skinless chicken breasts

Freshly ground black pepper

1 tablespoon (15 ml) unsalted butter

2 cups (500 ml) mixed baby greens

Adding herbs to ricotta is a good way to add natural plant antioxidants and flavor to a meal.

steps

1. Preheat the oven to 350° F (180° C).

2. Combine ricotta, herbs, and 1 tablespoon (15 ml) olive oil in a small bowl.

3. Cut a 3-inch (7.5-cm) pocket into the thickest part of each chicken breast. Using a spoon, stuff a quarter of the filling into each breast. Close each pocket with a toothpick. Season with pepper. Cover and refrigerate for 30 minutes.

4. Heat the butter and the remaining oil in a large skillet. Sauté the stuffed chicken breasts for 5 to 6 minutes on each side until brown.

5. Transfer chicken breasts to an ovenproof dish. Cover with aluminum foil and place in the oven for 10 more minutes. Serve over baby greens.

Nutrients per serving:

Calories: 303
Total Fat: 12 g
Saturated Fat: 3 g
Trans Fat: 0 g
Cholesterol: 118 mg
Sodium: 167 mg
Total Carbohydrates: 3 g
Dietary Fiber: 1 g
Sugars: 1 g
Protein: 44 g
Iron: 2 mg

Macronutrient Breakdown
5% Carbohydrates
59% Protein
36% Fat

Turkey Meatballs with Savory Sauce

4 servings

ingredients

Olive oil spray

1 pound (450 g) lean ground turkey

½ cup (125 ml) green onions, finely chopped

½ cup (125 ml) baby spinach, finely chopped

1 clove garlic, minced

½ cup (125 ml) dry bread crumbs

1 egg, lightly beaten

steps

1. Heat the oven to 400° F (200° C). Spray baking sheet with olive oil and set aside.

2. In a large bowl, mix all ingredients. Using a soup spoon, form meatballs.

3. Place meatballs on the prepared sheet and place in the oven. Bake for about 25 minutes, until meatballs are brown and cooked through.

4. Serve with dipping sauce.

Nutrients per serving:

Calories: 230
Total Fat: 11 g
Saturated Fat: 3 g
Trans Fat: 0 g
Cholesterol: 130 mg
Sodium: 115 mg
Total Carbohydrates: 9 g
Dietary Fiber: 2 g
Sugars: 1 g
Protein: 25 g
Iron: 2 mg

Macronutrient Breakdown
16% Carbohydrates
43% Protein
41% Fat

Savory Sauce

ingredients

1 tablespoon (15 ml) olive oil

1 tablespoon (15 ml) dark sesame oil

¼ cup (60 ml) low-sodium soy sauce

1 tablespoon (15 ml) rice vinegar

¼ cup (60 ml) packed dark brown sugar

1 teaspoon (5 ml) minced fresh ginger

steps

1. Mix all ingredients in a saucepan. Heat until boiling, reduce heat, and simmer for about 3 to 5 minutes until thickened.

2. Serve with turkey meatballs.

Nutrients per serving:

Calories: 110
Total Fat: 7 g
Saturated Fat: 1 g
Trans Fat: 0 g
Cholesterol: 0 mg
Sodium: 550 mg
Total Carbohydrates: 11 g
Dietary Fiber: 0 g
Sugars: 9 g
Protein: 1 g
Iron: 0 mg

Macronutrient Breakdown
39% Carbohydrates
5% Protein
56% Fat

Turkey, Artichoke, and Tomato Tapas

6 servings

ingredients

2 teaspoons (10 ml) olive oil

1 pound (450 g) turkey tenderloins, cut into 3/4-inch (2-cm) medallions

1 (6-ounce) (170-g) jar marinated artichoke hearts, drained, halved; liquid reserved

2 tablespoons (30 ml) balsamic vinegar

1/4 teaspoon (1 ml) dried oregano

1/4 teaspoon (1 ml) red pepper flakes

1 large clove garlic, minced

6 to 8 cherry tomatoes, halved

It's rumored that tapas originated because King Alfonso X of Spain had a disease that required him to eat small meals with sips of wine.

steps

1. Heat oil in a large nonstick skillet set over medium heat. Add turkey and sauté for 4 minutes per side, or until turkey is golden brown and no longer pink in center. A instant-read thermometer, inserted in thickest portion of tenderloin, should read 165° F (74° C).

2. In a medium bowl, combine artichoke liquid, vinegar, oregano, pepper flakes, and garlic. Fold turkey and artichokes into mixture. Cover and refrigerate overnight.

3. Before serving, fold in tomatoes.

Nutrients per serving:

Calories: 130
Total Fat: 5 g
Saturated Fat: 1 g
Trans Fat: 0 g
Cholesterol: 49 mg
Sodium: 112 mg
Total Carbohydrates: 4 g
Dietary Fiber: 1 g
Sugars: 1 g
Protein: 17 g
Iron: 1 mg

Macronutrient Breakdown
13% Carbohydrates
53% Protein
34% Fat

Don't Break Your Heart

Tomato and Basil Turkey Bundles

4 servings

ingredients

Olive oil cooking spray

¼ cup (60 ml) grated Parmesan cheese

¼ teaspoon (1 ml) no-added-salt Italian seasoning

¼ teaspoon (1 ml) freshly ground black pepper

1 pound (450 g) turkey cutlets

½ cup (125 ml) julienned fresh basil

2 Roma tomatoes, seeded and julienned

¼ cup (60 ml) seasoned bread crumbs

8 cups (2 L) mixed greens

¼ cup (60 ml) Italian dressing

June, not November, is National Turkey Month.

steps

1. Spray a 13- x 9-inch (33- x 23-cm) baking sheet with olive oil and set aside.

2. In a small bowl, combine cheese, Italian seasoning, and pepper. Sprinkle mixture evenly over one side of cutlets and top with basil. Divide tomatoes equally over cutlets. Roll cutlets up, jellyroll-style, to encase tomato and basil mixture. Spray each bundle with olive oil and coat with bread crumbs.

3. Place bundles, seam side down, on the prepared sheet. Bake for 20 to 25 minutes, or until a instant-read thermometer registers 165° F (74° C) and turkey is no longer pink in center.

4. Serve bundles on bed of mixed greens tossed with dressing.

Nutrients per serving:

Calories: 230
Total Fat: 8 g
Saturated Fat: 2 g
Trans Fat: 0 g
Cholesterol: 77 mg
Sodium: 324 mg
Total Carbohydrates: 9 g
Dietary Fiber: 3 g
Sugars: 3 g
Protein: 29 g
Iron: 3 mg

Macronutrient Breakdown
16% Carbohydrates
52% Protein
32% Fat

Grilled Turkey Fajitas with Salsa

4 servings

ingredients

1 pound (450 g) turkey cutlets

2 teaspoons (10 ml) olive oil

1 large green bell pepper, cut in very thin strips

8 (6-inch) (15-cm) corn tortillas

1 cup (250 ml) salsa*

1 cup (250 ml) chopped fresh cilantro

Fajitas debuted in 1969 at Otilia Garza's Round-up restaurant in the Rio Grand Valley.

Mexican cowboys invented the dish. They used throwaway meat items, such as skirt steak, from the ranches where they worked, to make "fajitas."

steps

1. Heat the grill on high. Pat turkey cutlets dry with paper towels. Grill over preheated flame, about 4 inches (10 cm) from heat, for 4 to 6 minutes per side, or until the turkey registers 165° F (74° C) on an instant-read thermometer.

2. While turkey is cooking, heat oil in a skillet set over medium heat. Add pepper strips and sauté until soft.

3. Warm tortillas according to package directions.

4. Slice turkey into ¼-inch (0.5-cm) strips.

5. To assemble, divide turkey strips and place in center of each tortilla. Cover with pepper strips and top with 2 tablespoons (30 ml) each salsa and cilantro. Fold and serve.

*See Viva Mexico Salsa recipe on page 34 or use store-bought.

Nutrients per serving:

Calories: 300
Total Fat: 5 g
Saturated Fat: 1 g
Trans Fat: 0 g
Cholesterol: 70 mg
Sodium: 373 mg
Total Carbohydrates: 34 g
Dietary Fiber: 3 g
Sugars: 7 g
Protein: 31 g
Iron: 2 mg

Macronutrient Breakdown
44% Carbohydrates
42% Protein
14% Fat

Turkey Breast with Honey-Mustard Glaze

6 servings

ingredients

1 (4- to 6-pound) (2- to 3-kg) turkey breast

½ teaspoon (2 ml) kosher salt

¼ teaspoon (1 ml) freshly ground black pepper

¼ cup (60 ml) honey

2 tablespoons (30 ml) Dijon mustard

Mustard seeds, one of the world's most ancient spices, are believed to be cultivated in India around 3000 BC.

Hippocrates wrote of mustard's medicinal properties as a relief, when applied topically, for muscle pain or toothache.

steps

1. Preheat the oven to 325° F (160° C).

2. Season interior and exterior of turkey breast with salt and pepper.

3. In a 13- x 9- x 2-inch (33- x 23- x 5-cm) pan, place turkey breast on a V-shaped rack. Roast, uncovered, for 1 to 2 hours, or until a instant-read thermometer registers 165° to 170° F (75° to 80° C) in the thickest part of breast.

4. Meanwhile, in a small bowl, combine honey and mustard. Brush glaze over breast during the final 20 minutes of cooking.

5. Remove from oven and allow turkey breast to stand for 10 minutes before carving.

Nutrients per serving:

Calories: 174
Total Fat: 1 g
Saturated Fat: 0 g
Trans Fat: 0 g
Cholesterol: 70 mg
Sodium: 336 mg
Total Carbohydrates: 13 g
Dietary Fiber: 0 g
Sugars: 12 g
Protein: 28 g
Iron: 1 mg

Macronutrient Breakdown
30% Carbohydrates
64% Protein
6% Fat

Don't Break Your Heart

Peppered Turkey Medallions with Chutney Sauce

4 servings

ingredients

1 pound (450 g) turkey tenderloins, cut into ¾-inch (2-cm) medallions

1 tablespoon (15 ml) mixed peppercorns

1 teaspoon (5 ml) unsalted butter

2 teaspoons (10 ml) olive oil, divided

2 tablespoons (30 ml) minced green onion

¼ cup (60 ml) turkey broth

2 tablespoons (30 ml) cooking wine

¼ cup (60 ml) prepared chutney

Chutney, typically made with fruit, vinegar, sugar, and spices, originated in India.

steps

1. Crush peppercorns in a spice grinder, food processor, or with a mortar and pestle. Pat peppercorns onto both sides of turkey medallions. Refrigerate for 30 minutes.

2. In a large nonstick skillet set over medium heat, sauté medallions in butter and 1 teaspoon (5 ml) olive oil for 4 to 5 minutes per side, or until no longer pink in center. Remove medallions from the skillet and keep warm.

3. Add remaining oil to the skillet and sauté onion for 30 seconds. Add broth and cook for 45 seconds to reduce liquid. Stir in cooking wine and cook for 1 to 2 minutes. Reduce heat to low and blend in chutney.

4. To serve, place turkey medallions on a warm dinner plate. Pour chutney sauce over medallions.

Nutrients per serving:

Calories: 231
Total Fat: 4 g
Saturated Fat: 1 g
Trans Fat: 0 g
Cholesterol: 73 mg
Sodium: 257 mg,
Total Carbohydrates: 18 g
Dietary Fiber: 1 g
Sugars: 10 g
Protein: 30 g
Iron: 2 mg

Macronutrient Breakdown
31% Carbohydrates
52% Protein
17% Fat

Turkey and Avocado in Orange Sauce

4 servings

ingredients

1 pound (450 g) turkey cutlets, cut into ½-inch (1-cm) strips

2 cloves garlic, minced

1 tablespoon (15 ml) unsalted butter

3 ounces (90 g) frozen orange juice concentrate, thawed

½ cup (125 ml) reduced-sodium chicken broth

1¼ teaspoons (6 ml) reduced-sodium Worcestershire sauce

2 teaspoons (10 ml) brown sugar

1 tablespoon (15 ml) cornstarch

2 tablespoons (30) cold water

1 avocado, peeled and cubed

1 (11-ounce) (312-g) can mandarin oranges, drained

8 ounces (225 g) cooked linguine

¼ cup (60 ml) almonds, toasted, for garnish

To prevent browning, sprinkle lemon juice on an already sliced avocado or keep the flesh in contact with the pit and store in a plastic bag.

steps

1. In a large skillet set over medium heat, sauté turkey and garlic in hot butter for 2 to 3 minutes, or until turkey is no longer pink.

2. Stir in orange juice concentrate, broth, Worcestershire sauce, and brown sugar; bring to a boil. Reduce heat and simmer 4 to 5 minutes.

3. In a small bowl, combine cornstarch and water. Stir into turkey mixture. Cook, stirring, until mixture is slightly thickened. Gently fold in avocado and oranges. Heat 1 minute.

4. To serve, spoon turkey mixture over linguine. Garnish with almonds.

Nutrients per serving:

Calories: 381
Total Fat: 13 g
Saturated Fat: 3 g
Trans Fat: 0 g
Cholesterol: 78 mg
Sodium: 127 mg
Total Carbohydrates: 34 g
Dietary Fiber: 5 g
Sugars: 17 g
Protein: 33 g
Iron: 3 mg

Macronutrient Breakdown
35% Carbohydrates
35% Protein
30% Fat

chapter 7

Wholesome Grains

Whole Grains of Truth

Whole grains are one of the easiest and most healthful ingredients to prepare.

*You need between three to seven servings of grain-based foods a day –
make at least half whole grains.*

*Decrease your risk of several illnesses, including heart disease and
diabetes, by eating whole grains instead of refined grains.*

Eating whole grains helps you take off the pounds and keep trim.

To get all the health and flavor benefits of whole grains, be adventurous and eat a variety.

Featured Nutrients

*The following nutrients in whole grains provide energy, help build strong bones and cartilage, boost the
immune system, and help protect cardiovascular health:*

*Protein, carbohydrates, fiber, phytochemicals, iron, magnesium, phosphorus, zinc, copper, manganese,
selenium, and B vitamins*

Whole grains contain all of the parts of the grain seed: the bran, germ, and endosperm. Whole grains can be processed into flour or cereal and, if they deliver 100 precent of the original kernel, are still considered whole grain.

Types of whole grains include:

- ♥ Amaranth
- ♥ Barley
- ♥ Buckwheat
- ♥ Corn
- ♥ Millet
- ♥ Oats

- ♥ Quinoa
- ♥ Rice (wild, brown)
- ♥ Rye
- ♥ Sorghum
- ♥ Teff

- ♥ Triticale
- ♥ Wheat (spelt, emmer, faro, einkorn, khorasan wheat, bulgur, cracked wheat, wheat berry)

Wheat originated in the Tigris and Euphrates river valley, near what is now Iraq.

Keep in mind that any of these grains are no longer whole if they are processed and the bran or germ is taken out. In fact, most grains consumed in America are of this refined type. Refined grains do not have the fiber or nutrients found in whole grains since much of the nutrition is contained in the bran and the germ of the kernel. Endosperm, such as white rice or white flour, is the part leftover after grains are processed into refined grains. While rich in carbohydrates, endosperm lacks much of the other nutrients. Manufacturers often add some of the vitamins back to white flour, called "enriched flour." The fiber and the natural antioxidants, however, are gone.

Don't Break Your Heart

Spotting Whole Grains

To make sure you're getting whole grains, keep an eye on the ingredients listed on the food label. Look for the word "whole" in the first few ingredients. For example, if a bread is primarily whole grain, it should list "whole wheat flour" or "whole rye flour" as its first ingredient. If it says "100% whole grain" on the package, it is also all whole grain.

The Whole Grains Council has a Whole Grain Stamp that may be on the package, which tells you that the product contains at least half a serving of whole grain. A 100% Stamp indicates the product is a full serving of whole grain. According to the U.S. Dietary Guidelines, we should consume at least half of our grains as whole grains. To keep your heart healthy, make most of your grains whole.

In the 2010 Dietary Guidelines for Americans, a serving of whole grain is defined as any of the following:

- ½ cup (125 ml) cooked brown rice or other cooked grain

- ½ cup (125 ml) cooked 100% whole-grain pasta

- ½ cup (125 ml) cooked hot cereal, such as oatmeal

- 1 ounce (25 g) uncooked whole grain pasta, brown rice, or other grain

- 1 slice 100% whole grain bread

- 1 very small (1 ounce) (25 g) 100% whole grain muffin

- 1 cup (250 ml) 100% whole grain ready-to-eat cereal

Be aware that the fiber content alone won't necessarily tell you if the product is whole grain since non-whole grain ingredients can be added to up the fiber content. The word "whole" or the Whole Grains Council Stamp is more reliable, though whole grain products almost always have more fiber than their refined counterparts, a good thing for health.

Whole Grains are Healthy

Whole grains are rich in fiber, vitamins, minerals, and plant nutrients that help prevent disease. People who eat whole grains also tend to have healthier body weights than those who do not. Including whole grains in a heart-healthy diet is a great idea for a number of reasons. Not only do populations that traditionally eat a lot of whole grains have lower rates of heart disease, the nutrients in whole grains can keep blood pressure lower. And as a rich source of fiber and more protein than refined grains, whole grains help with weight loss and maintenance, a good tactic for keeping the heart healthy.

Whole-Grain Cooking Tips

Most grains are prepared by placing them in a pan with water or broth, bringing the mixture to a boil, and then simmering until all the liquid is absorbed. Whole grains often take a bit more time to cook than their refined versions, so factor it in to your meal preparation time. However, there are some shortcuts you can take to cut down on the cook time.

- ♥ Presoak whole grains by letting them sit in the water for a few hours before cooking. Then add a little extra water just before you bring to a boil.

- ♥ Make large batches of whole grains and refrigerate up to 4 days or freeze in small containers for up to a month. Add a little water before you pop them in the oven to reheat or use in cold salads.

- ♥ Look for pre-cooked versions in the supermarket, such as quick cooking brown rice or quinoa. These are usually microwaveable to heat and serve in 90 seconds.

Cooking Whole Grains

(adapted from the Whole Grains Council)

To 1 cup (250 ml) of this grain:	Add this much water or broth:	Bring to a boil, then simmer for:	Amount after cooking:
Amaranth	6 cups (1.5 L)	15-20 minutes	2½ cups (625 ml)
Barley, hulled	3 cups (750 ml)	45-60 minutes	3½ cups (875 ml)
Buckwheat	2 cups (500 ml)	20 minutes	4 cups (1 L)
Bulgur	2 cups (500 ml)	10-12 minutes	3 cups (750 ml)
Cornmeal (polenta)	4 cups (1 L)	25-30 minutes	2½ cups
Kamut grain	4 cups (1 L)	soak overnight then cook 45-60 minutes	3 cups (750 ml)
Millet, hulled	hulled 2½ (625 ml)	25-35 minutes	4 cups (1 L)
Oats, steel cut	4 cups (1 L)	30 minutes	3 cups (750 ml)
Pasta, whole wheat	6 cups (1.5 L)	8-12 minutes (varies by size)	varies
Quinoa	2 cups (500 ml)	12-15 minutes	3+ cups (750 ml+)
Rice, brown or black	2½ cups (625 ml)	25-45 minutes (varies)	3 to 4 cups (750 ml to 1 L)
Rye	4 cups (1 L)	soak overnight then cook 45-60 minutes	3 cups (750 ml)
Sorghum	4 cups (1 L)	25-40 minutes	3 cups (750 ml)
Spelt berries	4 cups (1 L)	soak overnight then cook 45-60 minutes	3 cups (750 ml)
Wheat berries	4 cups (1 L)	soak overnight then cook 45-60 minutes	3 cups (750 ml)
Wild rice	3 cups (750 ml)	45-55 minutes	3½ cups (875 ml)

Only 5 percent of the world's crop of oats is consumed by humans. At one point, it was believed that oats were a diseased form of wheat.

Blackberries are packed with protective antioxidants called anthocyanins.

Oatmeal Pancakes with Berry Crush

4 servings

ingredients

Berry Crush

2 cups (500 ml) fresh or frozen blackberries or raspberries

¼ cup (60 ml) granulated sugar

¼ cup (60 ml) pure maple syrup, plus more if needed

Pancakes

1⅔ cups (400 ml) whole wheat flour

⅔ cup (150 ml) old-fashioned rolled oats

2 tablespoons (30 ml) granulated sugar

1 ¼ teaspoons (6 ml) low-sodium baking powder

¼ heaping teaspoon (1 ml) baking soda

¼ teaspoon (1 ml) fine sea salt or iodized salt

1 cup (250 ml) nonfat Greek yogurt, plus more

for garnish

1 cup (250 ml) nonfat milk

4 teaspoons (20 ml) unsalted butter, melted, plus more for the pan

2 large eggs

Vegetable oil cooking spray

steps

1. To make the Berry Crush, combine the berries and sugar in a medium bowl and mash slightly with a fork. Strain the juice into a small pot and reserve the berries.

2. Heat the juice over medium heat and simmer until it is thick, syrupy, and easily coats the back of the spoon, about 8 minutes. Remove from the heat and stir in the maple syrup. Cool slightly and pour over the berries. Adjust the sweetness with additional maple syrup, if needed. Set the syrup aside.

3. To make the pancakes, whisk together the flour, oats, sugar, baking powder, baking soda, and salt in a large bowl.

4. In a separate bowl, whisk together the yogurt, milk, melted butter, and eggs. Make a well in the center of the dry ingredients and whisk in the wet ingredients until well incorporated. The batter should be thick, with tiny bubbles on the surface.

5. Heat a cast-iron or nonstick skillet over medium heat until a drop of water sizzles when splashed on the pan. Spray the griddle with cooking spray.

6. Drop about ⅓ cup (75 ml) of batter per pancake onto the hot griddle, leaving about 1 inch (5 cm) or so between pancakes. When bubbles form around the edges, gently lift and flip the pancakes with a flexible spatula. Cook on the other side until the pancakes are golden brown around the edges, about 2 minutes. Don't worry if the first one doesn't come out perfect—just adjust your heat as needed.

7. Repeat, adding cooking spray to the pan as needed, until all the pancakes are cooked. Stack the pancakes and garnish with butter or additional Greek yogurt and a generous ladle of Berry Crush. Serve hot.

Cooking Tip: For evenly golden brown pancakes, go light on the butter in the pan and keep the heat on your griddle low. If you prefer a pancake with a crispier exterior and a golden rim, cook pancakes at slightly higher heat, using enough butter to sizzle and foam in the pan between each batch.

Nutrients per serving:

Calories: 501
Total Fat: 8 g
Saturated Fat: 4 g
Trans Fat: 0 g
Cholesterol: 105 mg
Sodium: 348 mg
Total Carbohydrates: 86 g
Dietary Fiber: 11 g
Sugars: 40 g
Protein: 21 g
Iron: 4 mg

Macronutrient Breakdown
69% Carbohydrates
17% Protein
14% Fat

Sweet Potato Waffles

4 servings

ingredients

Dry

1½ cups (375 ml) whole wheat flour

¼ cup (60 ml) packed brown sugar

1 tablespoon (15 ml) low-sodium baking powder

½ teaspoon (2 ml) ground cinnamon

Wet

3 eggs, at room temperature

1 cup (250 ml) nonfat milk

½ cup (125 ml) fat-free sour cream

½ cup (125 ml) sweet potatoes, baked and mashed

4 teaspoons (20 ml) unsalted butter, melted

⅓ cup (75 ml) pecans, finely chopped (optional)

Maple syrup, to taste (optional)

The 400 varieties of sweet potatoes come in a rainbow of colors, including orange, pink, purple, cream, and yellow.

Sweet potatoes, full of antioxidants, have a moderate glycemic index and have been shown to decrease inflammation.

steps

1. Preheat a waffle iron. Depending on the type of iron you have, you may need to lightly oil it.

2. Combine all of the dry ingredients in a large bowl and whisk them until well combined.

3. Separate the egg yolks from the whites, reserving both.

4. In a medium bowl, combine the milk, sour cream, mashed sweet potato, melted butter, and egg yolks. Whisk until well combined.

5. In a small bowl, beat the egg whites at high speed for about two minutes. Stiff peaks should form when you lift the beaters. Set aside.

6. Pour the wet ingredients over the dry ingredients. Whisk until well combined, but do not over mix. The batter should be nearly smooth.

7. Fold in the beaten egg whites. If you are adding the pecans, fold them in now.

8. The batter is now ready for your waffle iron. The amount of batter and cooking time will vary according to the size and temperature setting of your waffle iron. Serve hot with maple syrup on the side, if desired.

Cooking Tip: Sweet potatoes can be baked for 1 hour at 400° F (200° C) or cooked in a microwave until soft.

Nutrients per serving:

Calories: 473
Total Fat: 14 g
Saturated Fat: 4 g
Trans Fat: 0 g
Cholesterol: 151 mg
Sodium: 162 mg
Total Carbohydrates: 71 g
Dietary Fiber: 7 g
Sugars: 32 g
Protein: 16 g
Iron: 4 mg

Macronutrient Breakdown
60% Carbohydrates
14% Protein
26% Fat

Don't Break Your Heart

Oatmeal and Leek Risotto

4 servings (side dish)

ingredients

3 cups (750 ml) low-sodium chicken broth

1 cup (250 ml) quick cook oats

2 tablespoons (30 ml) grape seed oil

1 cup (250 ml) leeks

1 to 2 garlic cloves, thinly sliced

10 cherry tomatoes, quartered

5 fresh basil leaves, torn

1 teaspoon (5 ml) ground black pepper

2 tablespoons (30 ml) low-sodium Parmesan cheese, grated

steps

1. Bring chicken broth to a boil and add oats, return to a boil, and simmer for 5 minutes until cooked and creamy.

2. Meanwhile heat grape seed oil in a skillet over medium heat. Add leeks and garlic and sauté until soft. Add cherry tomatoes and basil and cook 1 minute.

3. Add oatmeal and Parmesan cheese to sautéed ingredients and season with pepper. Mix the ingredients over medium heat for 2 minutes and serve.

Known in Europe as "poor man's asparagus," leeks are part of the onion family.

Compared to onions, leeks have a subtle and sweet taste.

Nutrients per serving:

Calories: 175
Total Fat: 9 g
Saturated Fat: 1 g
Trans Fat: 0 g
Cholesterol: 5 mg
Sodium: 107 mg
Total Carbohydrates: 18 g
Dietary Fiber: 3 g
Sugars: 2 g
Protein: 6 g
Iron: 2 mg

Macronutrient Breakdown
41% Carbohydrates
14% Protein
45% Fat

Creamy Quinoa Pasta and Edamame Carbonara

6 servings

ingredients

Olive oil cooking spray

6 slices turkey bacon

4 egg yolks

½ cup (125 ml) nonfat plain Greek yogurt

½ cup (125 ml) Parmesan cheese, grated

½ teaspoon (2 ml) ground black pepper

2 cups (500 ml) frozen edamame, shelled

1 (16-ounce) (450-g) box pasta, or brown rice or multi-grain pasta

2 tablespoons (30 ml) half-and-half cream

¼ cup (60 ml) fresh basil leaves, torn or thinly sliced

steps

1. Preheat the oven to 425° F (220° C). Coat a cookie sheet with cooking spray.

2. Spread the turkey bacon on the sheet and bake 15 to 20 minutes, until the bacon is crisp. Chop and set aside. In a medium bowl, whisk the egg yolks, yogurt, Parmesan cheese, and pepper until smooth.

3. Place the edamame in a large colander and set it in the sink. Cook the quinoa in a stockpot according to the package instructions and drain. Add edamame to pasta in stockpot and place it over very low heat. Add the egg mixture and turkey bacon.

4. Toss the pasta about 1 minute, until the egg mixture evenly coats the pasta. Turn off the heat add the half-and-half and stir well. Top with basil and serve immediately.

Although quinoa is cooked and eaten as a grain and has similar nutrients, it is actually a seed and is related to beets, chard, and spinach.

Quinoa, an ancient grain, was sacred to the Incas, who referred to it as chisaya mama, or "mother of all grains."

Nutrients per serving:

Calories: 440
Total Fat: 11 g
Saturated Fat: 3 g
Trans Fat: 0 g
Cholesterol: 134 mg
Sodium: 304 mg
Total Carbohydrates: 68 g
Dietary Fiber: 7 g
Sugars: 3 g
Protein: 19 g
Iron: 5 mg

Macronutrient Breakdown
61% Carbohydrates
17% Protein
22% Fat

Buckwheat Risotto with Goat Cheese

4 servings

ingredients

2 tablespoons (30 ml) olive oil

⅓ cup (75 ml) minced yellow or sweet onions

½ teaspoon (2 ml) dried thyme leaves

1½ cups (325 ml) buckwheat groats

½ cup (125 ml) white wine

1 cup (250 ml) mixed frozen vegetables, thawed

5 cups (1.25 L) low-sodium vegetable stock, heated

2 ounces (60 g) goat cheese, crumbled

¼ cup (60 ml) fresh basil leaves, chopped

Buckwheat is a fruit seed, not a cereal grain.

A great alternative to rice, buckwheat makes delicious porridge.

Eating buckwheat can help keep cholesterol levels and blood pressure in check.

steps

1. Heat the oil in a 4-quart (4-L) saucepan over medium heat. Add the onions; sauté for 2 minutes, stirring often, until the onions are soft.

2. Add the thyme; heat for 1 minute to release the flavor.

3. Add the buckwheat; stir to coat the grains evenly with oil for 1 minute.

4. Add the wine; cook, stirring, until all of the liquid is absorbed.

5. Begin adding the hot stock, ½ cup (125 ml) at a time, stirring frequently. Wait until each addition is almost completely absorbed before adding the next ½ cup (125 ml). Reserve about ¼ cup (60 ml) of stock to add at the end, if needed. Stir frequently to prevent the buckwheat from sticking.

6. After approximately 20 minutes, when the buckwheat is *al dente* (firm, sticks to teeth), add the remaining stock and mixed vegetables, stirring to combine ingredients.

7. Add the goat cheese and basil. Stir and serve.

Nutrients per serving:

Calories: 230
Total Fats: 10 g
Saturated Fat: 3 g
Trans Fat: 0 g
Cholesterol: 7 mg
Sodium: 243 mg
Total Carbohydrates: 28 g
Dietary Fiber: 4 g
Sugars: 4 g
Protein: 7 g
Iron: 2 mg

Macronutrient Breakdown
49% Carbohydrates
12% Protein
39% Fat

Whole Grains with Cranberries, Squash, and Pecans

6 servings

ingredients

1 cup (250 ml) long-grain brown rice

2 cups (500 ml) low-sodium chicken stock

½ cup (125 ml) water

1 cup (250 ml) butternut or acorn squash, peeled, seeded, and cut into ¼-inch (0.5-cm) cubes

2 tablespoons (30 ml) olive oil

1 teaspoon (5 ml) fresh sage, chopped

Freshly ground black pepper, to taste

Olive oil cooking spray

4 strips turkey bacon, chopped

¼ cup (60 ml) leeks, half-moon cut and dark green part omitted

2 tablespoons (30 ml) pecan halves, toasted

2 tablespoons (30 ml) dried cranberries

Rice, first cultivated in the foothills of the Himalayas, can be traced back to at least 5000 BC.

steps

1. In a saucepan, combine the rice with the chicken stock and water and simmer, covered, for 40 to 45 minutes, until the liquid is absorbed. Reserve.

2. Meanwhile, preheat the oven to 400° F (200° C). Coat cubed squash with olive oil and sage. Season with salt and pepper to taste. Spread squash onto a baking sheet and roast for 5 to 6 minutes on each side. Remove and cool.

3. Spray a nonstick skillet with cooking spray and cook bacon. Add leeks and cook for 1 minute. Add pecans and cranberries and mix well. Serve immediately.

Nutrients per serving:

Calories: 236
Total Fats: 10 g
Saturated Fat: 2 g
Trans Fat: 0 g
Cholesterol: 7 mg
Sodium: 158 mg
Total Carbohydrates: 31 g
Dietary Fiber: 4 g
Sugars: 4 g
Protein: 6 g
Iron: 1 mg

Macronutrient Breakdown
52% Carbohydrates
10% Protein
38% Fat

Black Rice and Toasted Pecan Pilaf

6 servings (side dish)

ingredients

3 cups (750 ml) black rice

2 cups (500 ml) water

½ cup (125 ml) pecans, coarsely chopped

1 tablespoon (15 ml) chopped fresh dill

1 teaspoon (5 ml) fresh parsley, chopped

1 tablespoon (15 ml) unsalted butter, cut into small pieces

¼ teaspoon (1 ml) kosher salt

¼ teaspoon (1 ml) freshly ground pepper

Rice comes in a variety of colors, including red and black.

Legend has it that black rice, also called forbidden rice, was reserved for the emperors of China.

Black rice, a whole grain, is packed with antioxidants.

steps

1. In a saucepan, combine the rice with the water and simmer, covered, for 50 to 60 minutes, until the rice kernels are soft and chewy. Reserve.

2. Toast pecans in a dry skillet over medium heat for 3 to 5 minutes, until fragrant.

3. Add toasted pecans, herbs, butter, salt, and pepper to the reserved rice, stirring to combine. Serve.

Cooking Tip: Brown rice can be substituted for the black rice. Increase the water by ½ cup (125 ml) and decrease the cooking time to 40 to 45 minutes.

Nutrients per serving:

Calories: 196
Total Fats: 10 g
Saturated Fat: 2 g
Trans Fat: 0 g
Cholesterol: 5 mg
Sodium: 116 mg
Total Carbohydrates: 25 g
Dietary Fiber: 2 g
Sugars: 1 g
Protein: 3 g
Iron: 1 mg

Macronutrient Breakdown
51% Carbohydrates
6% Protein
43% Fat

Whole Wheat Margherita Pizza

6 servings

ingredients

Crust

1 package active dry yeast

1 teaspoon (5 ml) honey

1 cup (250 ml) lukewarm water

2 cups (500 ml) whole wheat flour

½ teaspoon (2 ml) salt

¼ cup (60 ml) wheat germ, toasted

Topping

2 cups (500 ml) low-sodium mozzarella cheese

4 medium tomatoes, chopped

5 fresh basil leaves, chopped

Americans consume about 3 billion pizzas each year.

The first pizza to use cheese, Pizza Margherita, was created in honor of Margherita of Savoy, the Queen consort of Italy.

steps

1. Preheat the oven to 350° F (180° C).

2. In a small bowl, dissolve the yeast and honey in water. Let stand until creamy, about 10 minutes.

3. In a large bowl, combine the flour, wheat germ, and salt. Make a well in the middle and add the honey and yeast mixture. Stir well to combine. Cover and set in a warm place to rise for a few minutes.

4. Roll dough on a floured pizza pan and poke a few holes in it with a fork.

5. Bake 5 to 10 minutes, or until desired crispiness is achieved.

6. Spread cheese, tomatoes, and basil on baked pizza crust and heat with broiler on low until cheese melts.

Nutrients per serving:

Calories: 281
Total Fats: 7 g
Saturated Fat: 3 g
Trans Fat: 0 g
Cholesterol: 20 mg
Sodium: 207 mg
Total Carbohydrates: 37 g
Dietary Fiber: 7 g
Sugars: 4 g
Protein: 18 g
Iron: 2 mg

Macronutrient Breakdown
53% Carbohydrates
25% Protein
22% Fat

Don't Break Your Heart

Apple Barley Bread

12 servings (1 loaf)

ingredients

1 cup (250 ml) uncooked barley

2 cups (500 ml) boiling water

1½ teaspoons (7 ml) instant yeast

1½ teaspoons (7 ml) salt

2 tablespoons (30 ml) milled flax, or 1 tablespoon (15 ml) vegetable oil

2 tablespoons (30 ml) wheat gluten flour

¼ cup (60 ml) powdered milk

2¾ cups (675 ml) whole wheat flour

½ cup (125 ml) chopped dried apples

steps

1. Place the barley in a bowl or in the bucket of a bread machine and pour the boiling water over it. Cool to lukewarm, about 20 minutes, and stir in the remaining ingredients, except the apples.

2. Stir, then knead, to make a soft, slightly sticky dough (or allow to go through the dough cycle of a bread machine). If you're kneading by hand and the dough is very sticky, allow it to rest for 15 minutes before adding more flour.

3. Add the apples at the end of the kneading process, or when indicated by the bread machine.

4. Let the dough rise, covered, for 1 hour, until it's puffy.

5. Turn the dough out onto a lightly greased work surface, knead gently, then form into a loaf or ball. Place on a greased or parchment-lined baking sheet or in a greased 9- x 5-inch (23- x 13-cm) loaf pan. Cover and let rise till almost doubled in bulk, 1 to 1½ hours.

6. Preheat the oven to 400° F (200° C) while dough is rising. Bake the bread for 35 to 40 minutes, until it's deep brown and sounds hollow when thumped on the bottom. An instant-read thermometer inserted into the center of the loaf will register 205° F (100° C).

7. When ready, remove the bread from the oven, allow to cool in the pan for 10 minutes, then turn it out and onto a rack to cool completely.

Cooking Tip: This bread can also be made with rolled oats in place of barley cereal or with a mix of both grains.

Barley is used to make beers and lagers, whiskey, breads, breakfast cereals, and soups, just to name a few.

Barley remnants have been found in Egyptian pyramids and the grain is portrayed in ancient glyphs dating back to about 3000 BC.

Studies show that foods high in fiber, such as barley, can help decrease the risk of heart disease.

Nutrients per serving:

Calories: 183
Total Fats: 2 g
Saturated Fat: 0 g
Trans Fat: 0 g
Cholesterol: 0 mg
Sodium: 305 mg
Total Carbohydrates: 35 g
Dietary Fiber: 7 g
Sugars: 3 g
Protein: 7 g
Iron: 2 mg

Macronutrient Breakdown
76% Carbohydrates
14% Protein
10% Fat

Whole Wheat Noodles and Salmon with Sun-Dried Tomatoes

4 servings

ingredients

10 ounces (300 g) salmon fillet

4 cups (1 L) whole wheat spaghetti, cooked

4 teaspoons (20 ml) olive oil

4 fresh basil leaves, chopped

½ cup (125 ml) reduced-fat feta cheese, crumbled

1 cup (250 ml) sun-dried tomatoes

More than 600 pasta shapes are produced worldwide.

steps

1. Preheat the oven to 425° F (220° C).

2. Place the salmon, skin side down, in a nonstick pan and bake until the salmon is cooked through, about 10 to 12 minutes.

3. Combine the remaining ingredients in a large saucepan and cook over medium heat for 5 minutes. Transfer to a serving platter, place salmon on top, and serve.

Nutrients per serving:

Calories: 353
Total Fats: 11 g
Saturated Fat: 3 g
Trans Fat: 0 g
Cholesterol: 30 mg
Sodium: 508 mg
Total Carbohydrates: 43 g
Dietary Fiber: 7 g
Sugars: 6 g
Protein: 22 g
Iron: 3 mg

Macronutrient Breakdown
49% Carbohydrates
25% Protein
26% Fat

Brown Rice Yeast Rolls

8 servings

ingredients

4 cups (1 L) all-purpose flour

2 to 3 cups (500 to 750 ml) whole wheat flour

½ cup (125 ml) cornmeal

2 packages active dry yeast

1 teaspoon (5 ml) salt

¼ teaspoon (1 ml) baking soda

2 cups (500 ml) water

½ cup (125 ml) honey

¼ cup (60 ml) butter, cubed

2 cups (500 ml) brown rice, cooked

Historians believe that ancient Egyptians accidentally invented leavened bread when they added yeast to wheat paste.

We can thank ancient Egyptians for our less nutritious "modern" bread. Refined white bread became popular there around 1000 BC.

steps

1. In a large bowl, combine 2 cups (500 ml) all-purpose flour, 2 cups (500 ml) whole wheat flour, cornmeal, yeast, salt, and baking soda. In a small saucepan, heat the water, honey, and butter to 120° F (60° C). Add to the dry ingredients and beat until smooth. Stir in the rice and enough remaining flour, starting with whole wheat flour, to form a soft dough.

2. Turn onto a floured surface; knead until smooth and elastic, about 6 to 8 minutes. Place in a greased bowl, turning once to grease the top. Cover and let rise in a warm place until doubled, about 1 hour.

3. Gently deflate dough. Turn onto a lightly floured surface; divide into 30 pieces. Shape each into a roll. Place 2 inches (5-cm) apart on greased baking sheets. Cover and let rise until doubled, about 30 minutes.

4. Bake at 375° F (190° C) for 12 to 15 minutes or until golden brown. Remove from pans to cool on wire racks.

Nutrients per serving:

Calories: 355
Total Fats: 5 g
Saturated Fat: 3 g
Trans Fat: 0 g
Cholesterol: 10 mg
Sodium: 260 mg
Total Carbohydrates: 70 g
Dietary Fiber: 5 g
Sugars: 13 g
Protein: 9 g
Iron: 3 mg

Macronutrient Breakdown
77% Carbohydrates
10% Protein
13% Fat

Whole-Grain Corn Muffins

12 servings (12 muffins)

ingredients

1½ cups (375 ml) medium-grind cornmeal

1 cup (250 ml) whole wheat pastry flour

1 tablespoon (15 ml) baking powder

2 tablespoons (30 ml) granulated sugar

½ teaspoon (2 ml) sea salt

1 egg, lightly beaten

1 cup (250 ml) low-fat milk

¼ cup (60 ml) vegetable oil

American Indians, who had been baking cornbread for thousands of years, introduced the settlers to this mainstay.

steps

1. Preheat the oven to 400° F (200° C). Grease a standard muffin pan and set aside.

2. Mix together the cornmeal, whole wheat pastry flour, baking powder, sugar, and salt. Add the milk, egg, and oil and blend until smooth, being careful not to over mix.

3. Spoon batter into the muffin tins about ¾ full. Bake for about 20 minutes. When done, tops of the muffins should spring back when tapped.

Nutrients per serving:

Calories: 151
Total Fats: 5 g
Saturated Fat: 1 g
Trans Fat: 0 g
Cholesterol: 16 mg
Sodium: 208 mg
Total Carbohydrates: 22 g,Dietary Fiber: 2 g
Sugars: 3 g
Protein: 4 g
Iron: 1 mg

Macronutrient Breakdown
58% Carbohydrates
11% Protein
31% Fat

Honey-Wheat Rolls

16 servings (16 rolls)

ingredients

1 packet active dry yeast

1 cup (250 ml) lukewarm water

¼ cup (60 ml) orange juice

¼ cup (60 ml) unsalted butter, cut into 6 pieces

3 tablespoons (45 ml) honey

1 cup (250 ml) unbleached all-purpose flour

2 cups (500 ml) whole wheat flour

1¼ teaspoons (6 ml) salt

⅔ cup (150 ml) instant mashed potato flakes

¼ cup (60 ml) nonfat powdered milk

Nutrients per serving:

Calories: 174
Total Fats: 4 g
Saturated Fat: 3 g
Trans Fat: 0 g
Cholesterol: 10 mg
Sodium: 255 mg,
Total Carbohydrates: 30 g
Dietary Fiber: 3 g
Sugars: 6 g
Protein: 5 g
Iron: 1 mg

Macronutrient Breakdown
69% Carbohydrates
11% Protein
20% Fat

steps

1. Dissolve yeast with a pinch of sugar in 2 tablespoons (30 ml) of lukewarm water. Let yeast and water sit at room temperature for 15 minutes until mixture has bubbled and expanded.

2. Combine the dissolved yeast with remainder of the water and the rest of the ingredients. Mix and knead everything together—by hand, mixer, or bread machine set on the dough cycle—till you've made a smooth dough. If you're kneading in a stand mixer, it should take about 5 to 7 minutes at second speed. In a bread machine (or by hand), it should form a smooth ball.

3. Place dough in a lightly greased bowl. Cover the bowl and allow dough to rise, at room temperature, till it's quite puffy but not necessarily doubled in bulk, about 90 minutes to 2 hours. Rising may take longer, especially if you've kneaded by hand. Give it enough time to become quite puffy.

4. While the dough is rising, lightly grease a 9- x 13-inch (23- x 33-cm) pan, or two 9-inch (23-cm) round cake pans.

5. Gently deflate dough and transfer it to a lightly greased work surface. Divide it into 16 pieces.

6. Shape each piece into a rough ball by pulling the dough into a very small knot at the bottom (think of a balloon with its opening knotted), then rolling it under the palm of your hand into a smooth ball.

7. Place rolls in the 9- x 13-inch (23- x 33-cm) pan, or put 7 rolls in each of the round cake pans, spacing them evenly; they shouldn't touch one another.

8. Cover the pans with lightly greased plastic wrap and allow rolls to rise for 1½ to 2 hours. They'll become very puffy and expand to touch one another. While the rolls are rising, preheat the oven to 350° F (180° C).

9. Bake rolls for 15 minutes. Tent them loosely with aluminum foil and continue to bake until they're mahogany-brown on top, but lighter colored on the sides, an additional 10 to 13 minutes.

10. Remove rolls from the oven. After 2 or 3 minutes, carefully transfer them to a rack. They'll be hot and delicate, so be careful. Serve warm, or at room temperature.

Pumpkin Bread Wreathes

16 servings in 2 (8-inch) (20-cm) wreaths

ingredients

2¾ cups (675 ml) unbleached all-purpose flour

2 cups (500 ml) whole wheat flour

1 teaspoon (5 ml) ground cinnamon

1 teaspoon (5 ml) ground ginger

¼ teaspoon (1 ml) ground cloves

⅓ cup (75 ml) packed brown sugar

⅓ cup (75 ml) crystallized ginger, diced (optional)

1½ teaspoons (7 ml) salt

1 tablespoon (15 ml) instant yeast

1 (15-ounce) (425-g) can pumpkin

2 large eggs

¼ cup (60 ml) canola oil

Botanically, pumpkins are fruits.

Illinois is the top pumpkin producing state in the U.S.

In colonial times, pumpkins were an ingredient in pie crusts and not fillings.

Pumpkins were once used for removing freckles and for treating snake bites.

steps

1. Combine all the ingredients and knead them—by hand, electric mixer, or bread machine—until you've made a smooth, somewhat sticky dough.

2. Transfer the dough to a lightly oiled bowl, cover the bowl with plastic wrap, and set it aside to rise for 1 to 1½ hours; it should have expanded somewhat, but won't be too puffy.

3. Turn the dough out onto a lightly greased surface, divide it in half, and divide each half into 3 pieces.

4. Roll each piece into an 18-inch (46-cm) log. Working with 3 logs at a time, make a braid, pinching the ends together. Coil the braid into a lightly greased 8- or 9-inch (20- or 23-cm) cake pan, shaping it into a wreath-like circle and pressing the ends together where they meet. Repeat with the remaining logs.

5. Cover both pans with lightly greased plastic wrap and let the wreaths rise for about 90 minutes, until they look puffy, though not doubled in bulk.

6. Bake the bread in a preheated 350° F (180° C) oven for 30 minutes, until lightly browned and an instant-read thermometer inserted into the center reads 190° F (88° C). Remove the wreaths from the oven and allow them to cool on a rack.

Nutrients per serving:

Calories: 198
Total Fats: 5 g
Saturated Fat: 1 g
Trans Fat: 0 g
Cholesterol: 23 mg
Sodium: 231 mg
Total Carbohydrates: 32 g
Dietary Fiber: 4 g
Sugars: 6 g
Protein: 6 g
Iron: 2 mg

Macronutrient Breakdown
65% Carbohydrates
12% Protein
23% Fat

Don't Break Your Heart

Quinoa with Pesto

4 servings

ingredients

1 cup (250 ml) quinoa

2 cups (500 ml) water

Pesto

3 cups (750 ml) packed fresh basil leaves

3 cloves garlic

½ cup (125 ml) grated Parmesan cheese

½ cup (125 ml) olive oil

¼ cup (60 ml) walnuts

½ cup (125 ml) chopped fresh parsley (optional)

steps

1. Boil the water and add the quinoa. Turn the heat to low and simmer 15 minutes, until the water is absorbed and the quinoa is cooked (a ring will form around the seeds).

2. Place pesto ingredients in a food processor and pulse until smooth.

3. Stir 2 tablespoons (30 ml) of the pesto into the quinoa. Store the remaining pesto in an airtight container and refrigerate.

The traditional method of preparing pesto is to use a mortar and pestle.

Nutrients per serving:

Calories: 265
Total Fats: 8 g
Saturated Fat: 1 g
Trans Fat: 0 g
Cholesterol: 1 mg
Sodium: 188 mg
Total Carbohydrates: 40 g
Dietary Fiber: 6 g
Sugars: 4 g
Protein: 9 g
Iron: 3 mg

Macronutrient Breakdown
60% Carbohydrates
13% Protein
27% Fat

chapter 8

Lean Legumes

Legumes of Truth

*Canned beans are convenient; just rinse off any added salt
or buy the no-salt-added varieties.*

*Meatless Mondays, a popular and healthy trend meant to encourage Americans to go vegetarian
at least one day a week, are good for your health and the planet.*

*Decrease your risk of several illnesses, including heart disease and cancer,
by eating legumes more often.*

Low in saturated fat and no cholesterol, legumes are a heart-healthy way to get protein.

U.S. Dietary Guidelines recommend eating at least 3 cups (750 ml) of beans per week.

Featured Nutrients

*The following nutrients in legumes provide energy, help build lean muscle,
and help protect cardiovascular health:*

*Protein, carbohydrates, fiber, phytochemicals, folate, manganese,
potassium, iron, phosphorous, copper, and magnesium.*

Legumes 101

Beans, lentils, and peas—A.K.A. legumes—are a culinary and health treasure waiting for Americans to sit up and take notice. They are a major source of protein in other countries, yet only 8 percent of Americans eat beans on any given day. The 2010 U. S. Dietary Guidelines recommend that Americans eat more beans. So powerful are these low-cost, nutrient-rich powerhouses that they are categorized as both a vegetable and a protein. Balanced with low-glycemic carbohydrates, protein, minerals, vitamins, antioxidants, and fiber, their combined nutrients work together to keep you satisfied longer and provide the nutrition you need for energy and exercise recovery. Plus, the fiber is mostly soluble, which is good for cardiovascular and intestinal health.

What Are Legumes?

Legumes are plants that produce pods with seeds inside. There are several different types of legumes. See the table on the facing page for types of legumes and typical uses.

Legume	Good for...
Adzuki beans	Soups and Asian dishes
Anasazi beans	Soups and Southwestern dishes; can replace pinto beans
Black beans	Soups, stews, and Latin American dishes
Black-eyed peas	Salads, casseroles, and Southern dishes
Chickpeas (also known as garbanzo beans)	Casseroles, salads, hummus, minestrone soup, and Spanish and Indian dishes
Fava beans	Stews
Lentils	Soups, stews, salads, and Indian dishes
Lima beans (also known as butter beans)	Succotash, casseroles, soups, and salads
Red kidney beans	Stews, salads, and chili
Soybeans	Snacks, salads, casseroles, and Asian dishes

Powerhouse Nutrition

A half cup (125 ml) of beans, peas, or lentils has about 100 calories, 7 grams of fiber, and 7 grams of protein. But wait, there's more; legumes are also rich in iron, zinc, magnesium, potassium, folic acid, phosphorus, and phytochemicals. And they are full of antioxidants, too. In a study of more than 100 common foods, the U.S. Department of Agriculture reported that 3 out of the top 5 foods with the most antioxidant capacity were beans.

Eat Your Legumes

Combining legumes with grains, such as rice and beans, creates a complete protein with all of the amino acids your body needs for proper function. Many cultures have been pairing legumes with grains for centuries. This approach allows people to effectively get all the needed protein without overly relying on animal foods.

Try and eat at least ½ cup (125 ml) to 1 cup (250 ml) of legumes a day. Here's why:

Heart Helper

Studies show that eating legumes 4 to 7 days a week can decrease cardiovascular disease by 22 percent and heart attacks by 38 percent. Choosing plant proteins can reduce dietary cholesterol and saturated fat intake, reduce the risk of heart disease, and even reverse heart disease.

Body Shaper

Nutrient-rich, high fiber foods are key to losing fat while maintaining and building muscle. A recent study showed that bean eaters weigh an average of 7 pounds less and have smaller waists than non-bean eaters. Because of the fiber, protein, and even their weight, legumes are satiating and can help you avoid overeating.

Energy Extender

A low-glycemic food packed with carbohydrates, fiber, and protein, legumes have staying power. They fill you up and take a while to digest, providing sustained energy between meals.

Exercise Booster

Protein, carbohydrates, antioxidants, vitamins, and minerals—nutrients needed to recover and rebuild after an intense bout of exercise--are all found in legumes. They help you to get the most out of your workout and empower your body to train again.

Gassy Tips

- When cooking beans, toss the soaking water and use fresh to decrease gas-producing sugars.

- Cook beans slowly to break down gassy sugars.

- Canned beans are less gassy.

- Take a digestive aid, such as Beano.

- Drink plenty of water.

Tips on Cooking Legumes

- Peas and lentils don't need to soak prior to cooking.

- Uncooked dry beans typically double in amount after cooking.

- Quick Soak Method: Cover the beans with 3 inches (7 cm) of water and bring to a boil for 1 minute.

- Let the sit covered for 1 hour. After soaking, toss the water and cook with fresh water, following the directions on the package.

- Traditional Soak Method: Soak dried beans for at least 8 hours (or overnight) with enough water to cover the beans. After soaking, toss the water and cook with fresh water, following the directions on the package.

- Freeze cooked legumes for later by rinsing in cold water; once cooled, drain well and freeze.

- Add acidic ingredients like tomatoes, vinegar, or juice at the end of cooking to avoid tough legumes or delayed cooking time.

Buying Legumes

- Buy dry, frozen, or canned beans.

- Look for BPA-free cans.

- Choose low-salt or no-salt-added canned beans.

Note: For convenience, the recipes below list canned or frozen beans as ingredients, but feel free to substitute dry-cooked packaged beans or cook dried beans in the recipes. Just replace the same amount of the beans as listed in the ingredients with your own cooked beans.

Sweet Potato with Baked Beans

2 servings

ingredients

1 cup (250 ml) no-salt-added navy beans, cooked

½ cup (125 ml) water

½ tablespoon (15 ml) molasses

1 teaspoon (5 ml) dark brown sugar

¼ cup (60 ml) chopped onion

2 medium sweet potatoes, cooked

Most Americans eat less than 1 cup (250 ml) of beans a week, less than ⅓ of the recommendation.

Navy beans are perfect for making baked beans.

One cup of cooked navy beans provides 76 percent of the recommended intake for fiber.

Sweet potatoes are native to South and Central America.

Sweet potatoes are not related to yams, an entirely separate species grown in the tropics.

steps

1. Combine navy beans, water, molasses, dark brown sugar, and onion in a saucepan; bring to a boil for 1 minute, then simmer for 10 minutes.

2. Meanwhile, pierce sweet potatoes and microwave them for 10 minutes.

3. Cut potatoes in half lengthwise. Add ½ cup (125 ml) of the navy bean mixture on top of each sweet potato.

Nutrients per serving:

Calories: 305
Total Fat: 1 g
Saturated Fat: 0 g
Trans Fat: 0 g
Cholesterol: 0 mg
Sodium: 60 mg
Total Carbohydrates: 65 g
Dietary Fiber: 15 g
Sugars: 18 g
Protein: 11 g
Iron: 4 mg

Macronutrient Breakdown
84% Carbohydrates
13% Protein
3% Fat

Don't Break Your Heart

Black Bean, Lentil, and Plantain Salad

2 servings

ingredients

½ cup (125 ml) no-salt-added black beans, cooked

¼ cup (60 ml) no-salt-added lentils, cooked

½ cup (125 ml) chopped plantain, cooked

½ cup (125 ml) chopped fresh or frozen mango

¼ cup (60 ml) finely chopped onion

2 tablespoons (15 ml) red wine vinegar

Sea salt, to taste (optional)

Lentils, known as pulses, are in the same family as peas, chickpeas, and fava beans.

Lentils are rich in protein, folate, and essential nutrients.

Lentils benefit the environment as a rotation crop, adding nitrogen back to the soil.

steps

Combine all ingredients in a salad bowl. Toss and serve.

Nutrients per serving:

Calories: 196
Total Fat: 0.5 g
Saturated Fat: 0 g
Trans Fat: 0 g
Cholesterol: 0 mg
Sodium: 7 mg
Total Carbohydrates: 40 g
Dietary Fiber: 8 g
Sugars: 14 g
Protein: 8 g
Iron: 3 mg

Macronutrient Breakdown
82% Carbohydrates
16% Protein
2% Fat

Black-Eyed Pea, Tomato, and Egg Salad

1 serving

ingredients

½ cup (125 ml) no-salt-added black-eyed peas, cooked

½ cup (125 ml) chopped tomatoes

1 hard boiled egg, chopped

2 tablespoons (30 ml) balsamic vinegar

1 tablespoon (15 ml) reduced-fat feta cheese

steps

Mix all ingredients and enjoy.

In the South, black-eyed peas, also called cow peas, are traditionally eaten as the first food of the new year to bring luck and prosperity.

Nutrients per serving:

Calories: 239
Total Fats: 7 g
Saturated Fat: 2 g
Trans Fat: 0 g
Cholesterol: 189 mg
Sodium: 203 mg
Total Carbohydrates: 28 g
Dietary Fiber: 6 g
Sugars: 10 g
Protein: 16 g
Iron: 3 mg

Macronutrient Breakdown
47% Carbohydrates
27% Protein
26% Fat

Don't Break Your Heart

Vegetable-Stuffed Peppers

6 servings

ingredients

6 large green bell peppers

1 (15-ounce) (425-g) can no-salt-added pinto beans, rinsed and drained

3 cups (750 ml) corn kernels

¾ cup (175 ml) grated low-sodium Cheddar cheese

2 teaspoons (10 ml) vegetable oil

½ cup (125 ml) minced onion

1 clove garlic, minced

¼ cup (60 ml) minced fresh parsley

⅛ teaspoon (0.5 ml) ground cayenne pepper

¼ teaspoon (1 ml) ground black pepper

Use red, yellow, and green peppers for added color and variety.

steps

1. Preheat the oven to 375° F (190° C). Set a pot of water to boil.

2. Cut off tops of green peppers, leaving an opening of about 2 inches (5 cm) in diameter. Remove seeds and inner ribs.

3. Immerse peppers in boiling water and cook for 5 minutes. Remove peppers and drain upside down on paper towels.

4. In a medium bowl, combine remaining ingredients and mix well. Place 2 cups (500 ml) of filling in each pepper.

5. Put peppers (filled side up) in a baking dish. Pour a little water into the bottom of the dish. Bake peppers for 20 minutes.

Nutrients per serving:

Calories: 172
Total Fats: 6 g
Saturated Fat: 3 g
Trans Fat: 0 g
Cholesterol: 14 mg
Sodium: 18 mg
Total Carbohydrates: 22 g
Dietary Fiber: 7 g
Sugars: 6 g
Protein: 9 g
Iron: 2 mg

Macronutrient Breakdown
51% Carbohydrates
19% Protein
30% Fat

Sun-Dried Tomato Hummus

8 servings

ingredients

1 cup (250 ml) no-salt-added chickpeas, cooked

2 sun-dried tomatoes

1 teaspoon (5 ml) fresh lemon juice

1 tablespoon (15 ml) olive oil

1 tablespoon (15 ml) rice vinegar

2 tablespoons (30 ml) water

Sea salt, to taste (optional)

To make your own sun-dried tomatoes, peel and slice ripe, firm Roma tomatoes. Add basil, cover with cheesecloth, and place in the sun for 1 to 2 days.

Hummus adds protein and fiber to your diet.

steps

Purée all ingredients using either a food processor or a handheld blender. Refrigerate in an airtight container.

Cooking Tip: Enjoy hummus as a dip with your favorite vegetables and as a spread on your favorite bread, crackers, or baked low-sodium chips.

Nutrients per serving:

Calories: 47
Total Fats: 2 g
Saturated Fat: 0 g
Trans Fat: 0 g
Cholesterol: 0 mg
Sodium: 13 mg
Total Carbohydrates: 5 g
Dietary Fiber: 1 g
Sugars: 1 g
Protein: 2 g
Iron: 0.5 mg

Macronutrient Breakdown
44% Carbohydrates
18% Protein
38% Fat

Don't Break Your Heart

Edamame Avocado Dip

8 servings

ingredients

1½ cups (375 ml) frozen edamame, shelled

¼ avocado, peeled and pit removed

1 tablespoon (15 ml) pimentoes

1 clove garlic

2 teaspoons (10 ml) fresh lemon juice

3 tablespoons (45 ml) water

⅛ teaspoon (0.5 ml) sea salt

Edamame are green immature soybeans picked in their pods before ripening.

steps

Purée all ingredients using either a food processor or a handheld blender. Refrigerate in an airtight container.

Nutrients per serving:

Calories: 43
Total Fats: 2 g
Saturated Fat: 0 g
Trans Fat: 0 g
Cholesterol: 0 mg
Sodium: 46 mg
Total Carbohydrates: 3 g
Dietary Fiber: 2 g
Sugars: 1 g
Protein: 3 g
Iron: 1 mg

Macronutrient Breakdown
29% Carbohydrates
29% Protein
42% Fat

Fudgy Black Bean Brownies

Makes 16 brownies

ingredients

1 (15-ounce) (425-g) can no-salt-added black beans, drained and rinsed

3 large eggs

3 tablespoons (45 ml) canola oil

¾ cup (175 ml) granulated sugar

½ cup (125 ml) unsweetened cocoa powder

1 teaspoon (5 ml) pure vanilla extract

½ teaspoon (2 ml) baking powder

½ cup (125 ml) mini semi-sweet chocolate chips, divided

Brazil grows more black beans than any other country.

Unlike most brownies, these provide protein and fiber.

steps

1. Preheat the oven to 350° F (180° C). Spray an 8- x 8-inch (20- x 20-cm) baking pan with nonstick cooking spray.

2. Place black beans in the bowl of a food processor and process until smooth and creamy.

3. Add the eggs, oil, sugar, cocoa powder, and vanilla.

4. Add ¼ cup (60 ml) chocolate chips and pulse a few times until the chips are incorporated.

5. Pour the batter into the prepared pan, smooth the top with a rubber spatula, and sprinkle with the remaining ¼ cup (60 ml) chocolate chips.

6. Bake for 30 to 35 minutes, or until the edges start to pull away from the sides of the pan and a toothpick inserted in the center comes out clean. Cool in the pan before slicing into 2-inch (5-cm) squares.

Nutrients per serving:

Calories: 126
Total Fats: 6 g
Saturated Fat: 2 g
Trans Fat: 0 g
Cholesterol: 35 mg
Sodium: 29 mg
Total Carbohydrates: 18 g
Dietary Fiber: 2 g
Sugars: 13 g
Protein: 3 g
Iron: 1 mg

Macronutrient Breakdown
56% Carbohydrates
9% Protein
35% Fat

Sweet Onion Apricot Lima Beans

8 servings

ingredients

1 (15-ounce) (425-cm) can no-salt-added baby lima beans, rinsed and drained

1 medium onion, sliced

1 cup (250 ml) sliced dried apricots

½ teaspoon (2 ml) salt

5 cups (1.25 L) water

½ cup (125 ml) honey

This dish can be served hot, as a side dish, or cold, as a relish.

Lima beans, named after the capital city of Lima, Peru, have been grown in Peru since 6,000 BC.

Lima beans are one of the most popular beans grown in home gardens.

steps

1. Combine beans, onion, apricots, salt, and water in a saucepan. Cover and simmer for 1 hour.

2. Add honey and simmer for 5 minutes longer. Serve as a hot dish or cold relish with turkey, chicken, or pork.

Nutrients per serving:

158, Total Fats: 0.5 g
Saturated Fat: 0 g
Trans Fat: 0 g
Cholesterol: 0 mg
Sodium: 163 mg
Total Carbohydrates: 38 g
Dietary Fiber: 3 g
Sugars: 29 g
Protein: 3 g
Iron: 2 mg

Macronutrient Breakdown
91% Carbohydrates
7% Protein
2% Fat

Falafel

4 servings

ingredients

1 (15-ounce) (425-g) can no-salt-added garbanzo beans, rinsed and drained

1 medium onion, coarsely chopped

¼ cup (60 ml) packed parsley leaves

2 cloves garlic, minced

½ teaspoon (2 ml) ground cumin

¾ teaspoon (4 ml) dried oregano leaves

1 tablespoon (15 ml) fresh lemon juice

Salt and pepper, to taste

1 cup (250 ml) bread crumbs

¼ cup (60 ml) raisins, chopped

1 egg yolk

Tomato-Cucumber Relish (see recipe on page 166)

Tuck falafel, a traditional Arab food, into pita bread or serve with a green salad.

Although typically associated with the Middle East, falafel originated in Egypt.

steps

1. In a food processor or blender, process garbanzo beans, onion, parsley, garlic, cumin, and oregano until smooth; season to taste with lemon juice, salt, and pepper. Stir in ½ cup (125 ml) bread crumbs, raisins, and egg yolk.

2. Form bean mixture into 16 patties, using about 2 tablespoons (30 ml) for each. Coat patties with remaining ½ cup (125 ml) bread crumbs.

3. Spray a large skillet set over medium heat with cooking spray; heat until hot. Cook falafel until browned on the bottom, about 2 to 3 minutes. Spray tops of falafel with cooking spray and turn; cook until browned on the bottom, about 2 to 3 minutes.

4. Arrange 4 falafel on each plate; serve with Tomato Cucumber Relish.

Nutrients per serving:

Calories: 281
Total Fats: 4 g
Saturated Fat: 1 g
Trans Fat: 0 g
Cholesterol: 45 mg
Sodium: 229 mg
Total Carbohydrates: 50 g
Dietary Fiber: 7 g
Sugars: 14 g
Protein: 12 g
Iron: 4 mg

Macronutrient Breakdown
71% Carbohydrates
17% Protein
12% Fat

Don't Break Your Heart

Tomato Cucumber Relish

4 servings

ingredients

½ cup (125 ml) chopped tomato

½ cup (125 ml) chopped cucumber

⅓ cup (75 ml) fat-free plain yogurt

½ teaspoon (2 ml) dried mint leaves (optional)

Salt and pepper, to taste

steps

In a small bowl, combine tomato, cucumber, yogurt, and mint leaves; season to taste with salt and pepper.

Relish, typically made up of chopped vegetables or fruits, is used to enhance the flavor of a staple food.

Nutrients per serving:

Calories: 281
Total Fats: 4 g
Saturated Fat: 1 g
Trans Fat: 0 g
Cholesterol: 45 mg
Sodium: 229 mg
Total Carbohydrates: 50 g
Dietary Fiber: 7 g
Sugars: 14 g
Protein: 12 g
Iron: 4 mg

Macronutrient Breakdown
71% Carbohydrates
17% Protein
12% Fat

Don't Break Your Heart

Black Bean and Walnut Burgers

Makes 8 burgers

ingredients

2 (15-ounce) (425-g) cans no-salt-added black beans, rinsed and drained

2 teaspoons (10 ml) ground cumin

1 tablespoon (15 ml) chili powder

¼ teaspoon (1 ml) ground cayenne pepper

½ cup (125 ml) brown rice, cooked

½ cup (125 ml) chopped walnuts

⅓ cup (75 ml) chopped red onion

¼ cup (60 ml) corn kernels

⅓ cup (75 ml) cornmeal

Guacamole (optional)

Chunky salsa (optional)

This vegan dish can be prepared ahead of time and grilled or pan-fried when ready to eat.

Beans are rich in oligosaccharides, a complex carbohydrate that tends to cause flatulence. Eating beans regularly, once or twice a week, reduces this unpleasant side effect.

steps

1. In a blender or a food processor, purée 2½ cups (625 ml) beans with cumin, chili powder, and cayenne pepper until smooth. Add rice, walnuts, onion, corn, and remaining beans; pulse 2 or 3 times to mix (mixture should be stiff but not dry). Add 2 to 3 tablespoons (30 to 45 ml) water to moisten, if necessary.

2. Cover and chill if making ahead. When ready to cook, divide mixture into 8 burgers. Dredge burgers in cornmeal. Chill 30 minutes (unless mixture has been made earlier and chilled).

3. Coat a nonstick pan or a grill with cooking spray. Cook burgers over medium heat for 4 minutes. Flip, and cook 4 minutes more, or until heated through.

4. Serve with guacamole and salsa, if desired.

Nutrients per serving:

Calories: 173
Total Fats: 6 g
Saturated Fat: 1 g
Trans Fat: 0 g
Cholesterol: 0 mg
Sodium: 26 mg
Total Carbohydrates: 25 g
Dietary Fiber: 7 g
Sugars: 2 g
Protein: 8 g
Iron: 3 mg

Macronutrient Breakdown
56% Carbohydrates
18% Protein
26% Fat

Southwest Lean Bean Scramble

1 serving

ingredients

3 large egg whites

1 tablespoon (15 ml) nonfat milk

1 tablespoon (15 ml) chopped green bell pepper

1 ounce (25 g) low-fat Cheddar cheese

¼ cup (60 ml) no-salt-added pink or kidney beans

1 tablespoon (15 ml) low-sodium salsa

1 tablespoon (15 ml) fat-free sour cream

This quick, spicy scramble fits in well with busy mornings. Multiply recipe and repeat cooking procedure for additional servings.

Today's American Southwestern cuisine originated with native tribes and was shaped by cowboys and Mexican influences.

steps

1. In a small bowl, mix egg whites, milk, bell pepper, cheese, and beans.

2. Coat a nonstick skillet set over medium heat with cooking spray.

3. Pour egg mixture into pan. Cook and stir until egg is cooked through. Serve with salsa and sour cream.

Nutrients per serving:

Calories: 182
Total Fats: 2 g
Saturated Fat: 1g
Trans Fat: 0 g
Cholesterol: 0 mg
Sodium: 402 mg
Total Carbohydrates: 16 g
Dietary Fiber: 4 g
Sugars: 4 g
Protein: 23 g
Iron: 2 mg

Macronutrient Breakdown
37% Carbohydrates
51% Protein
12% Fat

Don't Break Your Heart

Thai Chicken and Bean Wraps

4 servings

ingredients

8 ounces (225 g) boneless skinless chicken breast, cut into ½-inch (1-cm) pieces

2 cups (500 ml) small broccoli florets

½ medium onion, chopped

½ medium green bell pepper, chopped

1 tablespoon (15 ml) minced ginger, or 1 teaspoon (5 ml) ground

2 teaspoons (10 ml) minced garlic

1 (15-ounce) (425-g) can no-salt-added black beans or dark red kidney beans, rinsed and drained

Thai Seasoning (see recipe below)

8 (6-inch) (15-cm) corn tortillas

An authentic Thai dish should include four main seasonings: salty, sweet, sour, and spicy.

steps

1. Coat a wok or a large skillet set over medium heat with cooking spray; heat until hot. Add chicken and cook until browned, about 3 to 4 minutes. Add broccoli, onion, bell pepper, ginger, and garlic and stir-fry until crisp tender, about 5 minutes. Stir in black beans and Thai Seasoning; cook until hot, about 2 to 3 minutes.

2. Cover tortillas with a damp cloth and warm in a microwave for 45 seconds.

3. Spoon about ½ cup (125 ml) of the bean mixture in center of each tortilla. Roll up and serve immediately.

Thai Seasoning

Makes ¼ cup (60 ml)

ingredients

1 tablespoon (15 ml) reduced-sodium soy sauce

2 tablespoon (30 ml) grated lemon peel, or 1 tablespoon (15 ml) fresh lemon juice

2 tablespoons (30 ml) minced fresh cilantro

1 tablespoon (15 ml) reduced-fat peanut butter

1 tablespoon (15 ml) brown sugar

1 tablespoon (15 ml) crushed red pepper

steps

Mix together all ingredients.

Nutrients per serving:

Calories: 414
Total Fats: 12 g
Saturated Fat: 2g
Trans Fat: 0 g
Cholesterol: 0 mg
Sodium: 433 mg
Total Carbohydrates: 59 g
Dietary Fiber: 8 g
Sugars: 6 g
Protein: 20 g
Iron: 4 mg

Macronutrient Breakdown
56% Carbohydrates
19% Protein
25% Fat

Baja Quesadillas

6 servings (2 each)

ingredients

1 medium zucchini, cut in half lengthwise and sliced

1 cup (250 ml) sliced onion

1 teaspoon (5 ml) minced garlic

1 small jalapeno chili, minced

1 teaspoon (5 ml) ground cumin

1 (15-ounce) (425-g) can no-salt-added black beans, rinsed and drained

1 (15-ounce) (425-g) can no-salt-added pinto beans, rinsed and drained

1 cup (250 ml) chopped tomato

½ cup (125 ml) finely chopped fresh cilantro

12 (6-inch) (15-cm) whole wheat tortillas

¾ cup (175 ml) shredded reduced fat four-cheese Mexican blend

Mexican blend

Salt and pepper, to taste

Low-sodium salsa, as topping

Sour cream, as topping

Spicy is the tradition for foods in Baja California, Mexico.

steps

1. Preheat the oven to 450° F (230° C).

2. Spray a large skillet set over medium heat with cooking spray; heat until hot. Sauté zucchini, onion, garlic, jalapeno chili, and cumin until crisp tender, about 5 minutes.

3. Add beans to one side of the skillet; coarsely mash about half the beans. Mix beans, tomato, and cilantro into onion mixture and cook for 1 to 2 minutes.

4. Spoon ⅓ cup of the mixture on one side of each tortilla and sprinkle with 1½ tablespoons cheese. Fold tortillas in half and spray both sides with cooking spray.

5. Bake on a cookie sheet until browned and crisp, about 5 to 7 minutes.

6. Top quesadillas with salsa and sour cream.

Nutrients per serving:

Calories: 323
Total Fats: 4 g
Saturated Fat: 2 g
Trans Fat: 0 g
Cholesterol: 10 mg
Sodium: 363 mg
Total Carbohydrates: 57 g
Dietary Fiber: 11 g
Sugars: 5 g
Protein: 17 g
Iron: 5 mg

Macronutrient Breakdown
68% Carbohydrates
21% Protein
11% Fat

Don't Break Your Heart

chapter 9

Sensational Salads

Greens of Truth

The darker the salad green, the more nutrients it contains.

Some salad dressings can have as much as 100 calories and 250 milligrams of sodium per tablespoon. To keep calories and sodium in check, use flavored vinegars and fruit juices in your homemade dressings at a ratio of one to one with healthful plant oils, such as olive, walnut, sesame, and flax.

Instead of salad dressing, try small amounts of another flavorful fat, such as avocado, olives, nuts, or creamy goat cheese.

Be cautious of certain salad toppings, such as croutons, bacon bits, and fried noodles and the amounts used. High in calories, sodium, and fat, these toppings can add up if you're not careful with portion size.

Featured Nutrients

Leafy greens, like romaine, butter, Boston red leaf lettuce, spinach, and kale are rich in vitamins A, C, and K, folate, potassium, and magnesium, nutrients found to keep the cardiovascular system healthy and blood pressure down.

Adding fruits and vegetables to greens, as well as healthful fats and lean protein sources, increase the overall nutrition of your salad.

Sensational Nutrition

Packed with nutrients that won't pack on the pounds, leafy greens have fewer than 15 calories per serving, so they're a bonus for cardiovascular health. Adding lean protein to your salad such as fish, beans, or chicken breast, makes a filling, nutritious meal with a reasonable calorie count. Small amounts of flavorful, healthy fats can be very satisfying and balance out the nutritional profile of your salad. In fact, research shows that healthy fats help with the absorption of several nutrients found in vegetables, so including them is the best way to get optimal nutrition out of the salad.

The pigments that give fruits and vegetables their bright colors are loaded with healthful nutrients called phytochemicals. By eating a variety of color groups, you get an abundance of these protective nutrients. Each color represents a class of compounds that protects various systems in the body. A colorful plate means more protection for your health. Think of these different plant compounds as the branches of the military; each serves a purpose that protects a different region.

Make Your Salad a Rainbow

Start with a heaping bowl of greens and then add a rainbow of fresh toppings to ensure you're getting a variety of phytochemicals. Interestingly, studies show the more variety and color in your food, the more you will eat. When it comes to veggies, that's a great thing! Don't be afraid to venture into unusual fruits and veggies to include in your salad. You may find the new flavors change your take on the ho-hum typical garden salad and give your taste buds a new appreciation for this dieter's delight.

Here are some ideas to help you eat a rainbow:

Red

(rich in lycopene, quercetin):

tomatoes, watermelon, pink grapefruit, guava, red peppers, apples, cranberries, strawberries, radishes, pomegranates, beets, cherries

Orange and Yellow

(rich in beta carotene):

carrots, pumpkin, squash, mango, apricots, oranges, sweet potatoes, peaches, papaya, plantains, kumquats, tangerines

Green

(rich in lutein, zeaxanthin, beta carotene, sulforaphane, glucosinolates):

spinach, kale, broccoli, cabbage, Brussels sprouts, asparagus, chicory greens, collard greens, peppers, peas, zucchini, avocado, artichokes

Blue and Purple

(rich in anthocyanins, chlorogenic acid):

blueberries, blackberries, black raspberries, plums, eggplant

White, Brown, Black

(rich in organosulfur compounds, epicatechin, lentinan, apigenin):

garlic, onions, turnips, mushrooms, pears, potatoes, olives

Turkey and Bean Salad with Apricot-Ginger Dressing

6 servings

ingredients

12 cups (3 L) baby spinach

12 to 16 ounces (350 to 450 g) cooked turkey or chicken breast, cut into ½-inch (1-cm) cubes

1 (15-ounce) (425-g) can garbanzo beans, rinsed and drained

1 (15-ounce) (425-g) can black-eyed peas or navy beans, rinsed and drained

2 cups (500 ml) small broccoli florets

1 large sweet apple, such as Red Delicious, cored and cubed

⅓ cup (75 ml) dried cranberries or raisins

½ cup (125 ml) walnuts

1¼ cups (310 ml) Apricot-Ginger Dressing (see page 32)

Salt and pepper, to taste

Spinach has more than a dozen different flavonoid compounds, which are anti-inflammatory and anti-cancer.

One cup (250 ml) of spinach has 200 percent DV of vitamin K, a nutrient needed for strong bones.

steps

1. In a salad bowl, combine spinach, turkey or chicken, garbanzo beans, black-eyed peas or navy beans, broccoli, apple, cranberries or raisins, and walnuts; add Apricot-Ginger Dressing and toss to coat. Season to taste with salt and pepper.

2. Serve salad on large salad plates or in bowls.

Cooking Tip: For a tropical topping, prepare the dressing using mango chutney instead of apricot preserves or jam.

Nutrients per serving:

Calories: 502
Total Fats: 11 g
Saturated Fat: 1 g
Trans Fat: 0 g
Cholesterol: 64 mg
Sodium: 503 mg
Total Carbohydrates: 63 g
Dietary Fiber: 15 g
Sugars: 30 g
Protein: 38 g
Iron: 9 mg

Macronutrient Breakdown
50% Carbohydrates
30% Protein
20% Fat

Chicken, Bean, and Wild Rice Salad

6 servings

ingredients

1 (6-ounce) (170-g) package fast-cooking long grain and wild rice, cooked without spice packet and cooled

1 (15-ounce) (425-g) can light or dark red kidney beans, rinsed and drained

1 (15-ounce) (425-g) can black beans or pinto beans, rinsed and drained

1 (11-ounce) (300-g) can mandarin oranges, drained

1 cup (250 ml) frozen peas, thawed

1 cup (150 ml) Raspberry Vinaigrette (see page 34)

6 cups (1.5 L) baby spinach

1 (12- to 16-ounce) (350- to 450-g) broiled or grilled boneless, skinless chicken breast, sliced or cubed

1 (15-ounce) (425-g) can julienne beets, drained

½ cup (125 ml) coarsely chopped pecan halves, toasted (optional)

Salt and pepper, to taste

Beets are a unique source of betalains, phytonutrients that act as an antioxidant and help remove toxins from the body. They are found in the pigment that makes beets dark red.

steps

1. In a large bowl, combine rice, beans, orange segments, and peas; add ⅔ cup (150 ml) Raspberry Vinaigrette and toss. Season to taste with salt and pepper.

2. Arrange spinach on 6 plates. Spoon dressed salad on spinach and place chicken on top. Spoon beets to the side. Drizzle remaining ⅓ cup (75 ml) Raspberry Vinaigrette over beets and chicken. Sprinkle with pecans, if desired.

Cooking Tip: To cool rice quickly, spread cooked rice on a cookie sheet and refrigerate.

Nutrients per serving:

Calories: 611
Total Fats: 22 g
Saturated Fat: 3 g
Trans Fat: 0 g
Cholesterol: 64 mg
Sodium: 250 mg
Total Carbohydrates: 64 g
Dietary Fiber: 14 g
Sugars: 17 g
Protein: 39 g
Iron: 7 mg

Macronutrient Breakdown
42% Carbohydrates
26% Protein
32% Fat

Provençal Grilled Tuna Salad

4 servings

ingredients

4 (6-ounce) (170-g) tuna steaks, each about 1-inch (2-cm) thick

3 tablespoons (45 ml) white wine or broth

3 tablespoons (45 ml) olive oil

2 tablespoons (30 ml) red wine vinegar

½ teaspoon (2 ml) chopped fresh rosemary or 1/4 teaspoon (1 ml) dried

½ teaspoon (2 ml) ground black pepper

⅛ teaspoon (0.5 ml) salt

1 clove garlic, minced

6 cups (1.5 L) salad greens

1 cup (250 ml) cherry tomatoes, halved

½ cup (125 ml) each thinly sliced red and yellow bell peppers

Nonstick cooking spray

Tomatoes are a rich source of the anti-cancer nutrient lycopene.

There are hundreds of different tomato varieties.

steps

1. Place fish in a glass dish.

2. To make vinaigrette, combine wine or broth and next 5 ingredients in a jar with a tight fitting lid. Shake well.

3. Pour 2 tablespoons (30 ml) over fish, add garlic, and turn to coat. Marinate for 15 to 30 minutes, turning once. Reserve remaining vinaigrette for salad dressing.

4. Coat grill rack with cooking spray and place on grill to heat 1 minute. Place tuna on grill 4 to 6 inches (10 to 15 cm) over heat source. Cover with lid or tent with foil. Cook, turning once, until tuna begins to flake easily when tested with a fork, about 7 minutes. Discard marinade.

5. Meanwhile, arrange salad greens on 4 plates. Place hot tuna on greens and add cherry tomatoes and peppers.

6. Shake remaining vinaigrette and drizzle over salads.

Nutrients per serving:

Calories: 273
Total Fats: 11 g
Saturated Fat: 2 g
Trans Fat: 0 g
Cholesterol: 55 mg
Sodium: 158 mg
Total Carbohydrates: 8 g
Dietary Fiber: 2 g
Sugars: 2 g
Protein: 36 g
Iron: 2 mg

Macronutrient Breakdown
11% Carbohydrates
53% Protein
36% Fat

Salmon Waldorf Salad

4 servings

ingredients

½ cup (125 ml) light mayonnaise

¼ cup (60 ml) plain nonfat yogurt

¼ teaspoon (1 ml) lemon-pepper seasoning

½ teaspoon (2 ml) dried thyme

¼ teaspoon (1 ml) salt

2 (7½-ounce) cans (200-g) salmon, drained

2 ribs celery, diced

1 large apple, chopped

½ cup (125 ml) chopped walnuts

8 cups (2 L) chopped romaine lettuce

Eating walnuts, a good source of an omega-3 called ALA, may reduce blood pressure, likely due to the ALA content.

Walnuts are rich in a form of vitamin E that has been found to be protective to the cardiovascular health of men.

steps

1. In a small bowl, blend mayonnaise, yogurt, lemon-pepper seasoning, thyme, and salt.

2. In a separate bowl, combine salmon, celery, apple, walnuts, and lettuce.

3. Toss dressing with salad and serve.

Nutrients per serving:

Calories: 330
Total Fats: 20 g
Saturated Fat: 2 g
Trans Fat: 0 g
Cholesterol: 70 mg
Sodium: 567 mg
Total Carbohydrates: 13 g
Dietary Fiber: 5 g
Sugars: 11 g
Protein: 25 g
Iron: 2 mg

Macronutrient Breakdown
15% Carbohydrates
30% Protein
55% Fat

Colorful Caprese Salad with Avocado

4 servings

ingredients

¼ cup (60 ml) balsamic vinegar

1 tablespoon (15 ml) red wine vinegar

¼ cup (60 ml) extra-virgin olive oil

1 clove garlic, minced

2 cups (500 ml) cherry tomatoes, halved

5 fresh basil leaves, chopped

½ cup (125 ml) sliced low-sodium mozzarella

½ avocado

steps

Combine balsamic vinegar, red wine vinegar, olive oil, garlic, tomatoes, and basil and mix well. Refrigerate for at least 1 hour. Also refrigerate avocado to make it easier to dice and firmer for salad. Right before serving, add mozzarella and mix well. Dice avocado, add to salad, and serve immediately.

Avocados, high in heart-healthy monounsaturated fat, contain more potassium than a banana.

The Hass avocado is the only variety of avocado grown year-round.

Mexico grows the most avocados, with California in second place.

Because of their high amount of unsaturated fats, avocados are a great substitute for butter.

Nutrients per serving:

Calories: 227
Total Fats: 19 g
Saturated Fat: 4 g
Trans Fat: 0 g
Cholesterol: 9 mg
Sodium: 13 mg
Total Carbohydrates: 8 g
Dietary Fiber: 2 g
Sugars: 5 g
Protein: 6 g
Iron: 1 mg

14% Carbohydrates
11% Protein
75% Fat

Summery Spinach Salad

4 servings

ingredients

1 tablespoon (15 ml) pure maple syrup or brown sugar

2 tablespoons (30 ml) red wine vinegar

1 tablespoon (15 ml) extra-virgin olive oil

Freshly ground pepper, to taste

6 cups (1.5 L) baby spinach

2 cups (500 ml) sliced fresh strawberries

1 cup (250 ml) mandarin oranges

⅓ cup (75 ml) fresh chives, cut into 2-inch (5-cm) pieces

½ cup (125 ml) chopped almonds, toasted

¼ cup (60 ml) crumbled goat cheese

California and Texas grow the most spinach in the United States.

Leafy greens provide the most vitamins and minerals for less calories than any other vegetable.

steps

Whisk maple syrup or brown sugar, vinegar, oil, and pepper in a large bowl. Add spinach, strawberries, oranges, and chives; toss to coat. Divide the salad among 4 plates and top with almonds and goat cheese.

Cooking Tip: To toast chopped or sliced nuts, stir constantly in a small dry skillet over medium-low heat until fragrant and lightly browned, about 2 to 4 minutes.

Nutrients per serving:

Calories: 242
Total Fats: 17 g
Saturated Fat: 4 g
Trans Fat: 0 g
Cholesterol: 7 mg
Sodium: 112 mg
Total Carbohydrates: 16 g
Dietary Fiber: 5 g
Sugars: 12 g
Protein: 7 g
Iron: 3 mg

Macronutrient Breakdown
25% Carbohydrates
12% Protein
63% Fat

Don't Break Your Heart

Viva Mexico Salad

2 servings

ingredients

2 cups (500 ml) salad greens

1 cup (250 ml) baked low-sodium tortilla chips

1 cup (250 ml) black beans or pinto beans

½ cup (125 ml) sliced red bell peppers

½ cup (125 ml) sliced orange bell peppers

½ cup (125 ml) sliced green bell peppers

1 medium tomato, chopped

½ cup (125 ml) chopped, pitted ripe olives

1 medium avocado, peeled and sliced

Ground black pepper, to taste

3 tablespoons (45 ml) low-fat sour cream

3 tablespoons (45 ml) salsa (see page 34 for Viva Mexico Salsa recipe)

1 tablespoon (15 ml) chopped fresh cilantro

Cilantro, typically used in Mexican cuisine, is native to the Mediterranean and Asia Minor regions.

Cilantro and coriander come from the same plant. The leaves are cilantro and the seeds are coriander.

steps

1. Layer a shallow bowl with salad greens. Place tortilla chips on top of greens. Layer beans, bell peppers, tomato, olives, and avocado. Season with black pepper, to taste.

2. Top salad with dollops of sour cream and salsa. Sprinkle with cilantro.

Nutrients per serving:

Calories: 250
Total Fats: 10 g
Saturated Fat: 2 g
Trans Fat: 0 g
Cholesterol: 4 mg
Sodium: 281 mg
Total Carbohydrates: 32 g
Dietary Fiber: 10 g
Sugars: 5 g
Protein: 8 g
Iron: 2 mg

Macronutrient Breakdown
51% Carbohydrates
13% Protein
36% Fat

Fancy Fruit Salad

2 servings

ingredients

½ cup (125 ml) watermelon, scooped with a melon baller

1 banana, thinly sliced

½ cup (125 ml) chopped mango

1 cup (250 ml) red seedless grapes, halved

½ cup (125 ml) sliced strawberries

1 cup (250 ml) low-fat vanilla Greek yogurt

steps

Mix all ingredients and refrigerate for 2 hours.

Mangos, one of the world's most popular fruits, are related to cashews and pistachios.

To determine a mango's ripeness, don't look at the color. Red doesn't necessarily mean ripe. Give it a squeeze; it should give slightly.

A firm mango will ripen at room temperature in a few days.

Nutrients per serving:

Calories: 225
Total Fats: 1 g
Saturated Fat: 0 g
Trans Fat: 0 g
Cholesterol: 0 mg
Sodium: 49 mg
Total Carbohydrates: 41 g
Dietary Fiber: 4 g
Sugars: 34 g
Protein: 13 g
Iron: 1 mg

73% Carbohydrates
23% Protein
4% Fat

Roasted Sweet Potato Salad

4 servings

ingredients

Olive oil cooking spray

6 sweet potatoes, peeled and cubed

1 cup (250 ml) corn kernels

1 medium Vidalia onion, chopped

2 tablespoons (30 ml) apple cider vinegar

¼ cup (60 ml) plain Greek yogurt

1 teaspoon (5 ml) ground paprika

¼ cup (60 ml) pine nuts

Discovered by a farmer in Georgia in 1931, sweet Vidalia onions were not an instant success, as onions were expected to be hot.

Store a Vidalia onion by wrapping it in a paper towel and refrigerating.

steps

1. Preheat the oven to 400° F (200° C). Spray a baking sheet with cooking spray.

2. Spread 1 layer of sweet potatoes on the pan and spray with cooking spray (leave room on one side to later add pine nuts). Roast for 25 minutes.

3. Meanwhile, mix together all other ingredients, except pine nuts, and set aside.

4. Spray pine nuts with olive oil and add to pan for last 5 minutes of roasting.

5. Add roasted sweet potatoes and pine nuts to mixture and refrigerate for at least 1 hour to allow flavors to blend.

Nutrients per serving:

Calories: 286
Total Fats: 7 g
Saturated Fat: 1 g
Trans Fat: 0 g
Cholesterol: 0 mg
Sodium: 124 mg
Total Carbohydrates: 49 g
Dietary Fiber: 8 g
Sugars: 16 g
Protein: 7 g
Iron: 2 mg

Macronutrient Breakdown
68% Carbohydrates
10% Protein
22% Fat

Chicken Cutlet Salad with Strawberry Balsamic Dressing

4 servings

ingredients

1 cup (250 ml) Strawberry Balsamic Dressing (see page 35)

6 thin-sliced chicken cutlets (about 1 pound) (450 g)

⅓ cup (75 ml) corn meal

⅓ cup (75 ml) whole wheat flour

½ teaspoon (2 ml) salt

½ teaspoon (2 ml) ground black pepper

1 tablespoon (15 ml) canola oil

Salad

¼ cup (60 ml) pine nuts

2 cups (500 ml) Bibb lettuce

2 cups (500 ml) arugula

8 strawberries, sliced

¼ cup (60 ml) crumbled goat cheese

Strawberries are abundant in anti-inflammatory phytonutrients.

Eight large strawberries count as a 1-cup (250-ml) fruit serving.

steps

1. Pour ½ cup (125 ml) Strawberry Balsamic Dressing in a resealable plastic bag. Add chicken cutlets, seal, and refrigerate. Marinate for at least 30 minutes or overnight.

2. While chicken is marinating, toast pine nuts by placing in a nonstick pan set over medium heat. Toast until fragrant and reserve.

3. Heat the oven to 200° F (90° C). In a shallow bowl, combine corn meal, flour, salt, and pepper. Place a nonstick sauté pan over medium heat and add 1 tablespoon (15 ml) canola oil. Remove chicken from marinade, one piece at a time, place in corn meal mixture and turn to coat both sides of cutlet. Place first 3 pieces of coated chicken in the sauté pan and cook for 3 to 4 minutes per side, until browned. Repeat with last 3 pieces of chicken. Remove chicken to a platter and place in the oven to keep warm.

4. In a large bowl, combine lettuce, arugula, pine nuts, and remaining ½ cup (125 ml) of dressing. Toss well. Add strawberries and goat cheese. Divide salad among 4 large plates. Top each with 2 pieces of warm chicken and serve.

Nutrients per serving:

Calories: 434
Total Fats: 28 g
Saturated Fat: 5 g
Trans Fat: 0 g
Cholesterol: 50 mg
Sodium: 550 mg
Total Carbohydrates: 22 g
Dietary Fiber: 4 g
Sugars: 6 g
Protein: 24 g
Iron: 3 mg

Macronutrient Breakdown
20% Carbohydrates
22% Protein
58% Fat

Grilled Balsamic Vegetable Salad with Capers

8 servings

ingredients

1 small eggplant, sliced

6 firm plum tomatoes, sliced

2 zucchini, sliced in rounds

2 tablespoons (30 ml) olive oil, plus more if needed

2 cloves garlic, minced

1 tablespoon (15 ml) capers

½ teaspoon (2 ml) granulated sugar

2 tablespoons (30 ml) balsamic vinegar

steps

1. Coat the grill pan with 1 tablespoon (15 ml) olive oil.

2. Fit as many vegetables as you can cut-side down on the pan and cook for 1 to 2 minutes. Flip and cook an additional 1 to 2 minutes.

3. Continue grilling the rest of the vegetables, adding more olive oil to the pan as needed. Place grilled vegetables in a large bowl.

4. In smaller bowl, combine garlic, capers, sugar, vinegar, and 1 tablespoon (15 ml) olive oil. Add to vegetables and toss well.

Eggplant skin is rich in nasunin, a nutrient found to protect brain cells from oxidative damage.

Eggplants belong to the nightshade family of vegetables, which also includes tomatoes, sweet peppers, and potatoes.

Eggplants grow like tomatoes, hanging from vines several feet high.

Nutrients per serving:

Calories: 103
Total Fats: 6 g
Saturated Fat: 1 g
Trans Fat: 0 g
Cholesterol: 0 mg
Sodium: 73 mg
Total Carbohydrates: 12 g
Dietary Fiber: 5 g
Sugars: 6 g
Protein: 2 g
Iron: 1 mg

Macronutrient Breakdown
40% Carbohydrates
8% Protein
52% Fat

Julienned Salad in Ginger Plum Dressing

4 servings

ingredients

2 plums

¼ cup (60 ml) white wine vinegar

3 tablespoons (45 ml) canola oil

1 teaspoon (5 ml) minced ginger

½ teaspoon (2 ml) granulated sugar

Pinch salt and pepper

1 cup (250 ml) jicama, sliced julienne

1 large cucumber, sliced julienne

1 red or orange bell pepper, sliced julienne

1 cup (250 ml) sugar snap peas, sliced julienne

Jicama, a root vegetable that looks like a turnip, can be peeled and used raw in salads.

Peas are actually a legume and grow on vines.

steps

1. Slice plums in half, remove pit, and place in a pot of boiling water for 3 to 5 minutes. Drain and peel.

2. Place plums in a blender. Add vinegar, canola oil, ginger, sugar, salt, and pepper and purée to make the dressing.

3. Place julienned vegetables in a large bowl. Add dressing and toss to coat.

Nutrients per serving:

Calories: 155
Total Fats: 11 g
Saturated Fat: 1 g
Trans Fat: 0 g
Cholesterol: 0 mg
Sodium: 46 mg
Total Carbohydrates: 12 g
Dietary Fiber: 4 g
Sugars: 8 g
Protein: 2 g
Iron: 1 mg

Macronutrient Breakdown
31% Carbohydrates
5% Protein
64% Fat

Shrimp, Fennel, and Mandarin Oranges Over Frisee

8 servings

ingredients

¼ cup (60 ml), plus 2 tablespoons (30 ml) red wine vinegar

¼ cup (60 ml), plus 1 tablespoon (15 ml) olive oil

4 shallots, minced

¼ teaspoon (1 ml) ground black pepper

1 pound (450 g) large shrimp, cleaned and deveined

2 fennel bulbs

Juice of 1 lemon

2 heads frisee, torn into pieces

1 (11-ounce) (300-g) can mandarin oranges, drained

Frisee, sometimes called curly endive, is a type of chicory.

Frisee is slightly bitter but milder than other endives.

steps

1. Whisk ¼ cup (60 ml) vinegar, ¼ cup (60 ml) olive oil, shallots, and black pepper in a small bowl. Set aside.

2. Heat 1 tablespoon (15 ml) olive oil in a large skillet set on medium-high heat. Add shrimp and sauté for 2 to 3 minutes until cooked through. Remove from pan.

3. Add 2 tablespoons (30 ml) vinegar to the pan and deglaze over medium heat. Pour pan drippings over shrimp.

4. Cut fennel bulbs into ¼-inch (0.5-cm) slices. Toss fennel with lemon juice in a large salad bowl. Add frisee, mandarin oranges, and dressing and toss well. Top with shrimp and serve.

Nutrients per serving:

Calories: 179
Total Fats: 10 g
Saturated Fat: 1 g
Trans Fat: 0 g
Cholesterol: 67 mg
Sodium: 126 mg
Total Carbohydrates: 10 g
Dietary Fiber: 4 g
Sugars: 6 g
Protein: 12 g
Iron: 3 mg

Macronutrient Breakdown
23% Carbohydrates
27% Protein
50% Fat

Pan-Seared Scallops with Mango-Cherry Tomato Salsa and Herb Salad

4 servings

ingredients

1 pound (450 g) sea scallops

Pinch salt and pepper

Olive oil spray

1 mango, chopped

½ cup (125 ml) cherry tomatoes, chopped

2 scallions, chopped

½ yellow bell pepper, chopped

½ jalapeno chili pepper, chopped

1 tablespoon (15 ml) chopped fresh mint

1 teaspoon (5 ml) fresh lime juice

Juice of 1 lemon

1 clove garlic, minced

1 teaspoon (5 ml) mustard

3 tablespoons (45 ml) olive oil

4 cups (1 L) chicory, or, if chicory is too bitter, substitute baby spinach

steps

1. Season scallops with salt and pepper. Sear over high heat in a sauté pan coated with spray for 1 minute per side. Transfer to a plate and set aside.

2. In a small bowl, combine mango, tomatoes, scallions, bell pepper, jalapeno peppermint, and lime juice.

3. In another small bowl, whisk together lemon juice, garlic, mustard, and olive oil. Place greens in a large bowl and toss with lemon dressing.

4. Divide salad between 4 plates, top with scallops and mango salsa, and serve.

Chicory, a bitter herb, can be eaten as salad leaves.

Chicory is often mistakenly called curly endive, which is actually a different species.

When roasted and ground, chicory root can be used as a coffee substitute.

Nutrients per serving:

Calories: 338
Total Fat: 5 g
Saturated Fat: 1 g
Trans Fat: 0 g
Cholesterol: 84 mg
Sodium: 535 mg
Total Carbohydrates: 29 g
Dietary Fiber: 10 g
Sugars: 7 g
Protein: 45 g
Iron: 5 mg

Macronutrient Breakdown
34% Carbohydrates
53% Protein
13% Fat

Don't Break Your Heart

chapter 10

Super Soups

Warm and Cozy Truths

Starting a meal with a broth-based soup can cut the total calories consumed by about 100 calories. By filling up on this lower calorie choice, you're more likely to eat less of the calorie-rich entrée or dessert.

While soups are often full of healthful nutrients, such as vegetables, beans, and lean protein, they can still be high in sodium. Some canned varieties have more than ⅕ teaspoon (1000 mg) in 1 cup (250 ml).

You can keep the sodium count at a reasonable heart-healthy level by preparing your own soup, either from scratch or by starting with low-sodium canned broth.

Approach creamy soups with caution. They can provide more than 50 percent of a day's saturated fat.

Featured Nutrients

The sky's the limit when it comes to soup's nutritional benefits. Soups can be rich in all kinds of nutrients, depending on the ingredients used. Fruits, vegetables, beans, dairy, whole grains, meats, and fish are all common ingredients found in soups the world over. Thus soups can contain almost every nutrient available, including protein, carbohydrates, fat, fiber, minerals, vitamins, and phytochemicals. Additionally, soups are filling, which is a great way to stay satisfied and avoid overeating.

Super Soups

Soups are a great way to include vegetables, beans, whole grains, lean meats, and even fruits in a meal. Start with a low-sodium broth, such as chicken stock, beef stock, or vegetable stock. Add flavorful veggies, such as onions, carrots, celery, and garlic, season with herbs and spices, and sit down to enjoy a tasty and relatively low calorie meal.

Pump up the protein by adding a lean meat, fish, or poultry and some beans. Beans and other legumes are rich in folate, magnesium, potassium, thiamin, and fiber, nutrients known to be heart protective. In addition, beans do not have the saturated fat or cholesterol animal products have so they help keep arteries clear. Studies find that populations that eat the most legumes have lower rates of heart attacks than populations where consumption is low.

Soup and Sodium

Canned and prepared soups can be very high in sodium, so making your own is a great way to keep the salt in check. Make your own chicken, turkey, or beef stock using lean cuts of meat, skinless turkey, or chicken breast on the bone. Buy soup veggies in the produce section of the store, including garlic, onions, celery, carrots, and parsnips and use to flavor your stock. Natural sea salt may offer more flavor for less sodium than traditional iodized salt, so you can use less. Add small amounts of salt to the stock, let simmer, and taste before adding more; as the soup cooks flavors will become more pronounced and you may not need as much salt as you think.

Soups and Weight Control

Soups are often low in energy density, meaning they offer a high volume of food for few calories. Studies find that people consume a consistent volume of food, so if we can lower the calories in the foods we eat, while maintaining the volume, we will have an easier time maintaining or even losing weight. Research finds that when people are given a broth-based soup at the start of a meal, the total calories consumed during the meal are lower than when they don't have soup. In other words, people who fill up on low calorie soup don't have room for other higher calorie fare. Be careful of cream or cheese based soups, however; they can be loaded with saturated fat and calories. Since using broth-based soups to lose weight often results in better cholesterol, triglyceride, and blood pressure levels, this approach also protects cardiovascular health.

Strawberry Gazpacho

8 servings

ingredients

Strawberry Gazpacho

2 pounds (900 g) strawberries, hulled and chopped

¾ pound (350 g) plum tomatoes, chopped

1 cucumber, peeled, seeded, and chopped

3 cloves garlic, smashed

1 jalapeno pepper

½ cup (125 ml) sherry vinegar

Freshly ground black pepper, to taste

Jicama Salad

2⅔ cups (650 ml) jicama, peeled and julienned

1 bunch chives, cut in 1½-inch (4-cm) lengths

2 tablespoons (30 ml) extra-virgin olive oil

1 tablespoon (15 m) chopped fresh thyme

Freshly ground black pepper, to taste

½ cup (125 ml) goat cheese

The state of California produces over 1 billion pounds of strawberries a year.

steps

1. To make the soup, purée strawberries, tomatoes, cucumbers, garlic, jalapeño, and vinegar in a blender. Season with black pepper.

2. To make the salad, combine jicama, chives, olive oil, and thyme in a bowl and season with black pepper.

3. For each serving, mound ⅓ cup (75 ml) salad in the center of a soup plate. Carefully ladle 1 cup (250 ml) gazpacho around salad; top with 1 tablespoon (15 ml) goat cheese, formed into a ball.

Nutrients per serving:

Calories: 137
Total Fat: 7 g
Saturated Fat: 3 g
Trans Fat: 0 g
Cholesterol: 7 mg
Sodium: 62 mg
Total Carbohydrates: 13 g
Dietary Fiber: 5 g
Sugars: 8 g
Protein: 5 g
Iron: 1 mg

Macronutrient Breakdown
39% Carbohydrates
15% Protein
46% Fat

Don't Break Your Heart

Chunky Tuna Chowder

8 servings

ingredients

2 tablespoons (30 ml) trans-free margarine

½ cup (125 ml) chopped onion

2 cups (500 ml) water

1 (15-ounce) (425-g) can cannellini beans, drained and rinsed

1 cup (250 ml) peeled carrots cut in ½-inch (1-cm) pieces

½ cup (125 ml) sliced celery

½ cup (125 ml) corn kernels

1 bay leaf

½ teaspoon (2 ml) dried thyme

½ teaspoon (2 ml) dried basil

2 teaspoons (10 ml) garlic powder

½ teaspoon (2 ml) ground black pepper

2 cups (500 ml) nonfat milk, divided

1/4 cup (60 ml) all-purpose flour

2 (6-ounce) (170-g) cans tuna, drained

¼ cup (60 ml) fresh parsley, divided

About 70 percent of the canned tuna Americans consume is skipjack, also called light tuna. About 30 percent is albacore, also called white tuna.

steps

1. In a large saucepan, melt margarine and sauté onion until softened. Stir in the next 10 ingredients; bring to a boil. Reduce heat and simmer, covered, for about 10 minutes.

2. Meanwhile, gradually add ½ cup (125 ml) milk to flour in a small bowl. Stir until smooth and thick.

3. Add remaining milk to chowder. Gradually whisk in flour mixture; blend well.

4. Fold in tuna and half the parsley, heat through. Garnish with remaining parsley.

Nutrients per serving:

Calories: 147
Total Fat: 3 g
Saturated Fat: 1 g
Trans Fat: 0 g
Cholesterol: 17 mg
Sodium: 218 mg
Total Carbohydrates: 17 g
Dietary Fiber: 3 g
Sugars: 6 g, Protein: 13 g
Iron: 2 mg

Macronutrient Breakdown
47% Carbohydrates
35% Protein
18% Fat

Speedy Squash Soup

8 servings

ingredients

2 tablespoons (30 ml) trans-free margarine

1 large onion, chopped

½ teaspoon (2 ml) dried sage

2 Granny Smith apples

1 (15-ounce) (425-g) can low-sodium, fat-free chicken broth

¾ cup (175 ml) water

1 (12-ounce) (350-g) package frozen squash, thawed

2 teaspoons (10 ml) grated fresh ginger

1 cup (250 ml) firm tofu, cubed

½ cup (125 ml) nonfat milk

Squash's bright orange color indicates that it is rich in beta-carotene, an antioxidant that is also good for the eyes.

steps

1. Melt margarine in a medium saucepan set over medium heat. Add onion and sage and cook for 3 minutes. Reserve ¼ of 1 apple for garnish; peel, core, and finely chop remaining apples. Add to onion mixture with broth and water; heat to simmering. Cook, covered, for 12 minutes.

2. Add squash, ginger, and tofu to apple mixture; simmer, uncovered, for 10 minutes.

3. In a blender, purée mixture in two batches until smooth. Return to the pan, stir in milk, and reheat over low heat. (For a thinner soup, add a little more water or broth.) Ladle soup into serving bowls and garnish each with thin slices of reserved apple.

Nutrients per serving:

Calories: 102
Total Fat: 3 g
Saturated Fat: 1 g
Trans Fat: 0 g
Cholesterol: 1 mg
Sodium: 60 mg
Total Carbohydrates: 15 g
Dietary Fiber: 2 g
Sugars: 9 g
Protein: 4 g
Iron: 1 mg

Macronutrient Breakdown
58% Carbohydrates
16% Protein
26% Fat

Blueberry Soup

4 servings

ingredients

4 cups (1 L) blueberries

1 cup (250 ml) red wine

¼ cup (60 ml) honey

¼ cup (60 ml) nonfat vanilla

Greek yogurt, for garnish

steps

1. In a food processor, combine the blueberries, red wine, and honey. Purée until smooth; do not strain.

2. Garnish each soup bowl with 1 tablespoon (15 ml) yogurt.

Cooking Tip: Purple grape juice can be substituted for the red wine, if desired.

Red wine contains resveratrol, a phytonutrient found to reduce inflammation and to prevent blood clots and damage to blood vessels.

Since resveratrol comes from red and purple grapes, purple grape juice has similar benefits.

Nutrients per serving:

Calories: 208
Total Fat: 1 g
Saturated Fat: 0 g
Trans Fat: 0 g
Cholesterol: 0 mg
Sodium: 11 mg
Total Carbohydrates: 47 g
Dietary Fiber: 4 g
Sugars: 35 g
Protein: 3 g
Iron: 1 mg

Macronutrient Breakdown
90% Carbohydrates
6% Protein
4% Fat

Apple Fennel Soup

4 servings

ingredients

1 (15-ounce) (425-g) can low-sodium, fat-free chicken broth

2 cups (500 ml) water

½ cup (125 ml) white wine

2 Golden Delicious apples, peeled, cored, and chopped

1 cup (250 ml) thinly sliced carrots

1 small onion, thinly sliced

½ cup (125 ml) chopped fresh fennel

1 bay leaf

¼ teaspoon (1 ml) dried thyme

6 black peppercorns

Plain nonfat yogurt (optional)

The entire fennel plant—the bulb, leaves, and seeds—is edible, with its taste resembling licorice or anise.

A fennel bulb is crunchy like celery.

Fennel is an excellent source of fiber, folate, and potassium, all heart-protective nutrients.

steps

1. In a large pot, combine broth, water, wine, apples, carrots, onion, fennel, bay leaf, thyme, and peppercorns; heat to boiling. Reduce heat to simmer, cover, and cook for 20 minutes.

2. Strain soup, reserving liquid. Remove bay leaf from apple-vegetable mixture. In a blender or food processor, purée mixture; add reserved liquid and blend well. Reheat soup, if necessary. To serve, ladle into 4 soup bowls and top each with dollop of yogurt, if desired.

Nutrients per serving:

Calories: 119
Total Fat: 0 g
Saturated Fat: 0 g
Trans Fat: 0 g
Cholesterol: 2 mg
Sodium: 77 mg
Total Carbohydrates: 27 g
Dietary Fiber: 3 g
Sugars: 15 g
Protein: 3 g
Iron: 1 mg

Macronutrient Breakdown
90% Carbohydrates
10% Protein
0% Fat

Vietnamese Chicken Pho

4 servings

ingredients

6 cups (1.5 L) low-sodium chicken broth

4 scallions, roughly chopped

1 clove garlic, crushed

1 teaspoon (5 ml) minced fresh ginger

1½ teaspoon (7 ml) Chinese five spice powder

1 tablespoon (15 ml) granulated sugar

1 tablespoon (15 ml) Low-sodium soy sauce

⅛ teaspoon (0.5 ml) hot pepper sauce

½ teaspoon (2 ml) dark sesame oil

8 ounces (225 g) thin rice noodles

1 pound (450 g) chicken tenders, halved crosswise

1 cup (250 ml) firm tofu, cubed

1 cup (250 ml) chopped shiitake mushrooms

Juice of 1 lime

1 bunch watercress or arugula

1 cup (250 ml) fresh bean sprouts

1 small bunch fresh mint, leaves removed from stalks

1 small bunch fresh cilantro, leaves removed from stalks

Shiitake mushrooms contain lentinan, a nutrient which has shown potential effects against colorectal cancer in animal studies.

steps

1. In a large stockpot set over high heat, warm chicken broth. Add scallions, garlic, ginger, five spice powder, sugar, soy sauce, hot pepper sauce, and sesame oil; bring to a boil. Lower heat to medium-low and simmer for 15 minutes.

2. While broth simmers, place rice noodles in a large bowl and cover with hot water. Soak for 5 minutes, then drain, and set aside.

3. Place a fine-meshed sieve over a large bowl. Strain broth and discard solids that collect. Return strained broth to the saucepan and bring to a mild simmer over medium-high heat. Add chicken pieces and tofu; cook for 3 to 4 minutes. Add mushrooms and cook for another 2 minutes. Add lime juice.

4. Divide noodles evenly between 4 large soup bowls. Ladle broth over noodles. Top each bowl with a handful of watercress or arugula. Serve with bean sprouts and mint and cilantro leaves.

Nutrients per serving:

Calories: 119
Total Fat: 0 g
Saturated Fat: 0 g
Trans Fat: 0 g
Cholesterol: 2 mg
Sodium: 77 mg
Total Carbohydrates: 27 g
Dietary Fiber: 3 g
Sugars: 15 g
Protein: 3 g
Iron: 1 mg

Macronutrient Breakdown
90% Carbohydrates
10% Protein
0% Fat

Sweet and Spicy Tomato and Pepper Chicken Soup

8 servings

For a heartier meal, decrease the chicken broth to 1 cup (250 ml) and the soup becomes a stew.

ingredients

1½ pounds (675 g) boneless, skinless chicken thigh meat, cut into

1-inch (5-cm) cubes

2 tablespoons (30 ml) olive oil

2 Spanish onions, diced

4 carrots, peeled and thinly sliced

2 zucchini, sliced in rounds and halved

2 cloves garlic, minced

2 tablespoons (30 ml) chili powder

2 teaspoons (10 ml) garam masala

⅛ teaspoon (0.5 ml) ground nutmeg

⅛ teaspoon (0.5 ml) ground ginger

¼ teaspoon (1 ml) kosher salt

2 teaspoons (10 ml) brown sugar

1 (15-ounce) (425-g) can no-salt-added diced tomatoes

2 cups (500 ml) low-sodium chicken broth

¼ cup (60 ml) apple cider vinegar

1 (15-ounce) (425-g) can white beans, drained and rinsed

¼ cup (60 ml) chopped fresh parsley, for garnish

steps

1. Heat olive oil in a Dutch oven set over medium-high heat. When hot, add chicken and stir. Sauté, stirring often, for about 5 minutes, or until chicken is browned on all sides.

2. Add carrots, zucchini, and garlic. Reduce heat to medium and cook, stirring occasionally, for about 6 to 7 minutes, or until vegetables are softened. Add chili powder, garam masala, nutmeg, ginger, salt, and brown sugar. Sauté, stirring, for another 2 minutes.

3. Add tomatoes, broth, and vinegar and stir to combine. Raise heat to high and bring to a boil. Reduce heat, cover, and cook for about 25 to 30 minutes, or until chicken is tender and cooked through.

4. Add beans, stir, and cook for another 2 to 3 minutes, or until beans are heated through. Garnish with chopped parsley and serve.

Nutrients per serving:

Calories: 285
Total Fat: 10 g
Saturated Fat: 2 g
Trans Fat: 0 g
Cholesterol: 55 mg
Sodium: 228 mg
Total Carbohydrates: 28 g
Dietary Fiber: 6 g
Sugars: 10 g
Protein: 21 g
Iron: 3 mg

Macronutrient Breakdown
39% Carbohydrates
29% Protein
32% Fat

Miso Noodle Soup

8 servings

ingredients

2 tablespoons (30 ml) canola oil

2 leeks, white part only, split, rinsed, and sliced

2 cloves garlic, minced

1 bunch chard

2½ quarts (2 L) water

4 ounces (115 g) soba noodles

1 cup (250 ml) shelled edamame

2 tablespoons (30 ml) miso

1 cup (250 ml) shredded cooked chicken (optional)

2 scallions, thinly sliced, for garnish

Miso, a traditional Japanese seasoning, is made by fermenting soybeans.

Miso is high in protein and rich in vitamins and minerals.

In Asian cuisines, miso paste is often stirred into soups for flavor and added nutrition. Because it is high in sodium, just small amounts should be used.

steps

1. Heat oil in a large pot set over medium heat. Add leeks and garlic and cook, stirring occasionally, until softened.

2. Remove stalks and ribs from chard; set leaves aside. Coarsely chop stalks and ribs and add to the pot. Cook, stirring occasionally, until tender, about 8 to 10 minutes. Add water to the pot, increase heat, and bring to a boil. Reduce heat, and simmer until tender, about 10 minutes.

3. Add soba noodles and cook until tender, about 3 minutes.

4. Coarsely chop reserved chard leaves and add to soup along with edamame. Cook until leaves are wilted.

5. Bring soup to a boil. Put miso in a small bowl and add 1 cup (250 ml) soup liquid, whisking until miso is incorporated; set aside. Add shredded chicken, if using, to pot; heat through for about 2 minutes.

6. Stir miso mixture into soup. Garnish with scallions and serve immediately.

Nutrients per serving:

Calories: 155
Total Fat: 5 g
Saturated Fat: 1 g
Trans Fat: 0 g
Cholesterol: 15 mg
Sodium: 324 mg
Total Carbohydrates: 17 g
Dietary Fiber: 3 g
Sugars: 3 g
Protein: 11 g
Iron: 2 mg

Macronutrient Breakdown
43% Carbohydrates
28% Protein
29% Fat

Beef and Barley Vegetable Soup

8 servings

ingredients

Vegetable oil cooking spray

1 pound (450 g) lean ground chuck

1 quart (1 L) water

1 (15-ounce) (425 g) can no-salt-added stewed tomatoes

1 (6-ounce) (170-g) can low-sodium tomato-vegetable juice cocktail

⅓ cup (75 ml) barley

⅓ cup (75 ml) dried green split peas

½ cup (125 ml) chopped onion

1 cup (250 ml) low-sodium beef broth

¼ teaspoon (1 ml) ground black pepper

¼ teaspoon (1 ml) dried oregano

¼ teaspoon (1 ml) dried basil

1 bay leaf

¾ cup (175 ml) chopped celery, including leaves

½ cup (125 ml) sliced carrot

steps

1. Coat a large Dutch oven with cooking spray. Place over medium-high heat until hot. Add ground chuck and cook until browned, stirring to crumble meat.

2. Drain meat on paper towels and pat dry. Wipe pan drippings from the Dutch oven with a paper towel.

3. Return meat to the Dutch oven. Add water, tomatoes, vegetable juice, barley, split peas, onion, beef broth, black pepper, oregano, basil, and bay leaf.

4. Bring mixture to a boil. Cover, reduce heat, and simmer for 45 minutes.

5. Stir in celery and carrots. Cover and simmer for 30 minutes.

6. Remove and discard bay leaf. Serve soup hot.

Nutrients per serving:

Calories: 183
Total Fat: 6 g
Saturated Fat: 2 g
Trans Fat: 0 g
Cholesterol: 37 mg
Sodium: 102 mg
Total Carbohydrates: 17 g
Dietary Fiber: 5 g
Sugars: 5 g
Protein: 15 g
Iron: 3 mg

Macronutrient Breakdown
37% Carbohydrates
33% Protein
30% Fat

Rocky Mountain Soup

6 servings

ingredients

1 teaspoon (5 ml) canola oil

½ pound (225 g) boneless pork loin, cut into ½-inch (1-cm) cubes

1 cup (250 ml) thinly sliced carrots

1 cup (250 ml) sliced potatoes

2 tablespoons (30 ml) onion soup mix

2 tablespoons (30 ml) granulated sugar

Ground black pepper, to taste

1 quart (4 L) water

2 (15-ounce) (425-g) cans no-salt-added crushed tomatoes

¼ teaspoon (1 ml) dried oregano

Hot pepper sauce, to taste

steps

1. Heat oil in a Dutch oven. Add pork and cook, stirring occasionally, until browned.

2. Add remaining ingredients and bring to a boil, reduce heat to simmer, cover, and cook gently for 30 to 45 minutes.

Nutrients per serving:

Calories: 146
Total Fat: 2 g
Saturated Fat: 1 g
Trans Fat: 0 g
Cholesterol: 20 mg
Sodium: 263 mg
Total Carbohydrates: 21 g
Dietary Fiber: 4 g
Sugars: 11 g
Protein: 11 g
Iron: 2 mg

Macronutrient Breakdown
58% Carbohydrates
30% Protein
12% Fat

chapter 11

Delicious Drinks

Drips of Truth

Keep calorie-laden drinks to a minimum and eat your calories instead.

Tea adds flavor and nutrition to water without adding calories.

Limit fruit juice to no more than a 4-ounce (115-ml) serving once a day.

Boost nutrients and flavor by adding fruit to your water.

Make water your beverage of choice to avoid drinking your calories.

Featured Nutrients

Drinks provide hydration and can provide energy and, depending on the beverage, a wide variety of nutrients. For example, orange juice provides vitamin C, potassium, folic acid, vitamin B6 and thiamin. Nonfat milk provides protein, vitamin D, vitamin B12, riboflavin, vitamin A, calcium, phosphorus, zinc, potassium, and magnesium.

Choosing the Right Drinks

Water should be first and foremost at the top of your beverage list, with tea and coffee next for low calorie drink choices. These drinks should make up most of your beverage consumption for the day. For nutrient-rich drinks, skim milk and 100 percent fruit juice top the list. Save these calorie and nutrient-rich drinks for a few times a day. Skim milk is a great way to add protein and nutrition to a meal. Be aware that 4 ounces (115 ml) of 100 percent fruit juice can take the place of one fruit serving once a day. For a lower calorie juice, try 100 percent vegetable juice, but keep tabs on the sodium content, which is higher than fruit juice.

Added sugar is the biggest problem with the majority of drinks people choose, so make sure to limit drinks with added sugars. Different types of milk, such as almond, soy, and hemp can contain high levels of added sugars to help with taste. Read the label and make sure that sugar is not one of the first ingredients.

Heart-Healthy Drinks

Many beverages benefit our cardiovascular system, such as tea, orange juice, Concord grape juice, pomegranate juice, acai juice, and moderate amounts of red wine. Additionally, moderate alcohol intake may have some heart-healthy benefits. Most of these drinks are rich in antioxidants and other key nutrients, such as potassium, which benefit our cardiovascular system. The key to including these drinks for their health benefits is to watch the calories that can expand your waistline. Remember that juices and teas can also be added to your favorite recipes as marinades or rubs.

Cranberry Green Tea

6 servings

ingredients

1½ quarts (1500 ml) water

1½ cups (375 ml) whole cranberries

1 cup (250 ml) granulated sugar

½ cup (60 ml) orange juice

¼ cup (60 ml) fresh lemon juice

1 tablespoon (15 ml) ground cloves

½ teaspoon (2 ml) ground cinnamon

1 cinnamon stick

2½ teaspoons (12 ml) matcha green tea
 (available in health stores, some grocery stores, and tea stores)

Green teas pair well with fruit, fish, as well as with many cheeses, including Brie and Camembert.

Preliminary research suggests that vitamin C helps the body absorb the healthy flavonoids found in green tea.

steps

1. Combine water and cranberries in a large pot. Bring to a boil, reduce heat, and let bubble for 30 minutes.

2. Add remaining ingredients except for matcha.

3. Cover and steep for 1 hour.

4. Add matcha during the last 2 minutes of steeping.

Nutrients per serving:

Calories: 157
Total Fat: 0 g
Saturated Fat: 0 g
Trans Fat: 0 g
Cholesterol: 0 mg
Sodium: 20 mg
Total Carbohydrates: 40 g
Dietary Fiber: 2 g
Sugars: 36 g
Protein: 0 g
Iron: 0 mg

Macronutrient Breakdown
100% Carbohydrates
0% Protein
0% Fat

Refreshing Raspberry Green Tea

2 servings

ingredients

1 pint raspberries

¼ cup (60 ml) granulated sugar

2 cups (500 ml) water

1 bag green tea or 1 tablespoon (15 ml) loose in infuser

Ice

Raspberries give this already healthful drink an extra antioxidant and a vitamin C punch.

steps

1. In a saucepan, add raspberries, sugar, and 1 cup (250 ml) water and bring to a boil. Reduce heat and simmer for 4 minutes.

2. Meanwhile, heat remaining water to 175° F (80° C) and steep tea for 2 to 3 minutes.

3. Strain raspberry mixture into green tea, add a few ice cubes, and refrigerate. Serve chilled.

Nutrients per serving:

Calories: 180
Total Fat: 1 g
Saturated Fat: 0 g
Trans Fat: 0 g
Cholesterol: 0 mg
Sodium: 9 mg
Total Carbohydrates: 43 g
Dietary Fiber: 10 g
Sugars: 32 g
Protein: 2 g
Iron: 0 mg

Macronutrient Breakdown
95% Carbohydrates
4% Protein
1% Fat

Heart-Healthy Hot Cocoa

1 serving

ingredients

1 cup (250 ml) nonfat milk

3 tablespoons (45 ml) unsweetened cocoa powder

¼ teaspoon (1 ml) pure vanilla extract

¼ teaspoon (1 ml) ground cinnamon

8 drops stevia

Marshmallow (optional)

Dark and decadent, this drink gives you the heart-healthy benefits of cocoa with less fat and calories than in a chocolate bar.

Cinnamon may help manage blood sugar levels.

steps

In a saucepan, heat milk to just about boiling. Add cocoa powder and mix well. Add remaining ingredients and stir to mix. Pour into a mug and add marshmallow, if desired.

Nutrients per serving:

Calories: 129
Total Fat: 2 g
Saturated Fat: 1 g
Trans Fat: 0 g
Cholesterol: 5 mg
Sodium: 106 mg
Total Carbohydrates: 20 g
Dietary Fiber: 6 g
Sugars: 13 g
Protein: 9 g
Iron: 2 mg

Macronutrient Breakdown
61% Carbohydrates
27% Protein
12% Fat

Sunny Sips

1 serving

ingredients

4 ounces (115 g) orange juice

4 ounces (115 g) plain soy milk

steps

Add soy milk to orange juice, mix, and enjoy.

This simple recipe tastes like an old-fashioned creamsicle.

Blending soy milk with orange juice adds protein and nutrients.

Nutrients per serving:

Calories: 111
Total Fat: 2 g
Saturated Fat: 0 g
Trans Fat: 0 g
Cholesterol: 0 mg
Sodium: 62 mg
Total Carbohydrates: 18 g
Dietary Fiber: 1 g
Sugars: 13 g
Protein: 4 g
Iron: 0 mg

Macronutrient Breakdown
66% Carbohydrates
16% Protein
18% Fat

Pomegranate White Tea Spritzer

1 serving

ingredients

2 ounces (57 g) pomegranate juice

6 ounces (170 g) water

1 bag white tea or 1 tablespoon (15 ml) loose in infuser

1 teaspoon (5 ml) fresh lime juice

Splash of club soda

Ice

Pomegranates are native to the region from Iran to the Himalayas in Northern India.

Grenadine is made from pomegranate syrup.

steps

1. Heat 1 cup water to 175° F (80° C) and steep tea for 2 to 3 minutes.

2. Mix steeped tea with rest of ingredients, refrigerate until chilled, and serve over ice.

Nutrients per serving:

Calories: 37
Total Fat: 0 g
Saturated Fat: 0 g
Trans Fat: 0 g
Cholesterol: 0 mg
Sodium: 12 mg,
Total Carbohydrates: 9 g
Dietary Fiber: 0 g
Sugars: 8 g
Protein: 0 g
Iron: 0 mg

Macronutrient Breakdown
100% Carbohydrates
0% Protein
0% Fat

Blueberry Baselito

1 serving

ingredients

4 basil leaves

2 teaspoons (10 ml) granulated sugar

2 tablespoons (30 ml) sparkling water

1½ ounces (45 g) frozen blueberries

Crushed ice

2 tablespoons (30 ml) fresh lime juice

1½ ounces (45 g) light rum

2 blueberries, for garnish

The anthocyanins in blueberries have anti-inflammatory properties that help protect against diseases such as cancer, heart disease, diabetes, and Alzheimer's disease.

steps

1. Combine basil leaves and sugar in an old-fashioned glass and add sparkling water. Muddle ingredients lightly with a pestle. Add blueberries, crush, and mix a second time.

2. Fill the glass ⅔ full with crushed ice. Add lime juice and rum and stir well. Spear 2 blueberries onto a small skewer. Garnish glass with skewer.

Tip: Blueberry Baselito is delicious with or without rum.

Don't Break Your Heart

Nutrients per serving:

Calories: 144
Total Fat: 0 g
Saturated Fat: 0 g
Trans Fat: 0 g
Cholesterol: 0 mg
Sodium: 8 mg
Total Carbohydrates: 12 g
Dietary Fiber: 1 g
Sugars: 8 g
Protein: 0 g
Iron: 0 mg

Macronutrient Breakdown
100% Carbohydrates
0% Protein
0% Fat

Cucumber Lime Green Tea

1 serving

ingredients

¼ cup (60 ml) sliced cucumber

½ lime

⅔ cup (150 ml) water

1 green tea bag or 1 tablespoon (15 ml) loose in holder

steps

1. Heat water to 175° F (80° C) and steep tea for 2 to 3 minutes.

2. Add lime juice and cucumber. Drink either warm or chilled.

Cucumbers, a member of the gourd family, are similar to melons, squash, and pumpkins

Nutrients per serving:

Calories: 15
Total Fat: 0 g
Saturated Fat: 0 g
Trans Fat: 0 g
Cholesterol: 0 mg
Sodium: 20 mg
Total Carbohydrates: 5 g
Dietary Fiber: 0 g
Sugars: 1 g
Protein: 0 g
Iron: 0 mg

Macronutrient Breakdown
100% Carbohydrates
0% Protein
0% Fat

Blueberry Tomato Shooter

4 servings

ingredients

1 pound (450 g) ripe tomatoes

2 teaspoons (10 ml) canola oil

1 small red pepper, chopped

4 teaspoons (20 ml) packed brown sugar

2½ cups (625 ml) fresh blueberries

Salt, to taste

¼ cup (60 ml) grated Parmesan cheese, for garnish

Fresh cilantro leaves, for garnish

Blueberries are divided into two species, wild, or low bush, and farmed, or high bush. Both types offer multiple health benefits.

steps

1. Make a small *X* in bottom of each tomato and plunge into a pot of boiling water. Blanch for 1 minute. Remove with a slotted spoon and run under cold water. Remove skin from tomatoes, place on a cutting board, and quarter tomatoes.

2. Heat oil in a large skillet set over medium-high heat. Add tomatoes and pepper. Cook, stirring, for about 5 minutes, or until vegetables begin to soften. Add brown sugar and cook for about 5 minutes. Add blueberries and cook until softened. Scrape into a food processor or blender and purée until smooth. Add salt to taste.

3. Place 1-tablespoon (15-ml) mounds of Parmesan cheese in a nonstick skillet set over medium heat. Fry each side until golden brown. Remove and let cool.

4. Spoon Blueberry Tomato Shooter in 4 glasses and garnish with Parmesan fries and cilantro before serving.

Tip: The shooter can be served either hot or cold. Spike with vodka or gin, if desired.

Nutrients per serving:

Calories: 171
Total Fat: 6 g
Saturated Fat: 2 g
Trans Fat: 0 g
Cholesterol: 10 mg
Sodium: 16 mg
Total Carbohydrates: 24 g
Dietary Fiber: 4 g
Sugars: 17 g
Protein: 7 g
Iron: 0 mg

Macronutrient Breakdown
55% Carbohydrates
15% Protein
30% Fat

chapter 12

Simple Shakes and Smoothies

Smoothies and Shakes of Truth

What's the difference between shakes and smoothies? Smoothies are fruit-based, while shakes are typically made with dairy products.

Both smoothies and shakes are a great way to pack in healthy ingredients.

Keeping the sugar and calories in check when adding smoothies to your day is a must. Limit calories to 400 or fewer.

Finding new combinations of fruits and vegetables for your smoothies will help keep a variety of nutrients in your diet.

Stick with wholesome, nutrient-rich ingredients when making smoothies instead of relying on artificial supplements.

Featured Nutrients

Smoothies and shakes made with fruits, vegetables, and legumes are high in phytochemicals called polyphenols, as well as vitamin C, potassium, folate, and fiber – all important for cardiovascular health. Dairy and soy ingredients increase the protein content and add bone and muscle building nutrients, such as calcium, vitamin D, phosphorus, iron, copper, and manganese. As a bonus, carbohydrates and energizing nutrients, such as B6, give you the necessary energy to workout or simply to enjoy the day.

Making Smoothies and Shakes: What You Should Know

The right ingredients are what makes smoothies and shakes (S&S) a great addition to your day. In order to whip up a S&S at any time, make sure to have plenty of fresh or frozen vegetables and fruits on hand, as well as juices and a dairy source such as yogurt or milk. A blender is also a must. We recommend using an immersion blender for the easiest clean-up. Just toss all the ingredients into a glass and immerse the handheld blender to mix the ingredients.

Smoothies and shakes can be incorporated into your diet at any time of the day. Sip one for a quick and nutritious breakfast or as a recovery drink after a workout. One of their best uses is to help you recover after exercise. In this case, you would want to drink your S&S within an hour after your workout so your body can get the nutrients it needs while it is at its maximum recovery stage. For post-workouts, we recommend adding a scoop of natural whey protein to your drink to boost muscle building and recovery.

To boost the nutritional value of your smoothies and shakes, try adding some of the following ingredients.

- *Ground chia seeds*
- *Ground flaxseeds or flax oil*
- *Matcha (concentrated finely-ground green tea)*
- *Wheat germ*
- *Whey protein*
- *Wheatgrass*

When choosing whey protein, go with the most natural option. The ingredient deck on the back of the packaging should list just a few items, such as whey protein concentrate and isolate. Stay away from artificial sugars and flavors and added fats (total fat should be no more than 1 gram). Also, cholesterol and sodium should be lower than 50 milligram each.

Smoothies and shakes can come at a cost, though—a calorie cost. A rule of thumb is to limit a serving to 400 calories or fewer; otherwise, along with all the great nutrition, you will also start packing on the pounds. When deciding to add a shake or smoothie to your health regimen, make sure to replace current calories with your new drink calories. For example, a peanut butter and jelly sandwich is about 400 calories. So, you might replace this type of food with a 400-calorie smoothie or shake. Your goal is to add nutrition to your day, not calories. And a slimmer waistline naturally helps to take care of your cardiovascular system.

Many of the ingredients and ingredient combinations in S&S may help burn fat. Preliminary research shows that having plenty of calcium in your fat cells helps your cells burn more fat. Additionally, flavonoids and vitamin C may work together to help the body use fat more efficiently as an energy source, while protein and dairy together may help banish belly fat. All in all, S&S are a great and easy way to combine nutrient-rich ingredients to add nutrition to your day.

Sunny Breakfast Shake

2 servings

ingredients

½ navel orange, peeled

2 mandarin oranges, peeled

½ cup (125 ml) fresh or frozen strawberries

8 ounces (225 g) orange juice

1 teaspoon (5 ml) matcha green tea (available in health stores, some grocery stores, and tea stores)

1 scoop whey protein isolate powder (available in health and nutrition stores)

½ cup (125 ml) plain low-fat yogurt

1 cup (250 ml) ice

steps

Process all ingredients in a blender until smooth. Serve immediately.

Flavonoids and vitamin C in green tea, strawberries, and citrus help keep the body from storing fat, break down fat cells, and burn fat more efficiently.

Matcha is concentrated green tea finely ground into a powder. Just 1 teaspoon (5 ml) contains as many flavonoids as 10 cups (2 L) of green tea.

Combining citrus and green tea helps the body naturally absorb more of the flavonoids found in green tea.

Nutrients per serving:

Calories: 206
Total Fat: 2 g
Saturated Fat: 0 g
Trans Fat: 0 g
Cholesterol: 2 mg
Sodium: 71 mg
Total Carbohydrates: 30 g
Dietary Fiber: 4 g
Sugars: 20 g
Protein: 17 g
Iron: 1 mg

Macronutrient Breakdown
59% Carbohydrates
32% Protein
9% Fat

Peanut Butter Shake

1 serving

ingredients

6 ounces (170 g) nonfat milk

½ banana

¼ cup (60 ml) nonfat or reduced-fat cottage cheese

1 tablespoon (15 ml) reduced-fat peanut butter

1 scoop whey protein isolate powder (available in health and nutrition stores)

Honey, to taste (optional)

½ cup (125 ml) ice

steps

Process all ingredients in a blender until smooth. Serve immediately.

Milk, cottage cheese, and whey protein are some of the richest sources of essential branched-chain amino acids (BCAAs). These special amino acids are key to maintaining, building, and repairing muscle.

Peanut butter adds heart-healthy fats, while arginine, an amino acid, and flavonoids increase blood flow and help maintain vascular health.

Nutrients per serving:

Calories: 360
Total Fat: 7 g
Saturated Fat: 2 g
Trans Fat: 0 g
Cholesterol: 9 mg
Sodium: 480 mg
Total Carbohydrates 36 g
Dietary Fiber: 3 g
Sugars: 24 g
Protein 42 g
Iron 1 mg

Macronutrient Breakdown
38% Carbohydrates
45% Protein
17% Fat

Pineapple Perk

1 serving

ingredients

1 cup (250 ml) pineapple (fresh or frozen, no sugar added)

½ banana

¼ cup (60 ml) firm tofu

1 scoop whey protein isolate powder (available in health and nutrition stores)

¼ cup (60 ml) water

½ cup (125) ice

steps

Process all ingredients in a blender until smooth. Serve immediately.

Pineapple contains bromelain, a natural anti-inflammatory enzyme.

Bananas, a low to medium glycemic food, help maintain balanced blood sugar levels.

Nutrients per serving:

Calories: 305
Total Fat: 3 g
Saturated Fat: 0 g
Trans Fat: 0 g
Cholesterol: 6 mg
Sodium: 43 mg
Total Carbohydrates: 38 g
Dietary Fiber: 4 g
Sugars: 24 g
Protein: 33 g
Iron: 2 mg

Macronutrient Breakdown
50% Carbohydrates
42% Protein
8% Fat

Mango Vanilla Crush

2 servings

ingredients

1 large mango or 1 cup (250 ml) frozen mango chunks

½ cup (125 ml) vanilla low-fat yogurt

1 scoop whey protein isolate powder (available in health and nutrition stores)

1 teaspoon (5 ml) psyllium powder (made from psyllium seed husks)

2 ounces (57 g) water

1 cup (250 ml) ice

steps

Process all ingredients in a blender until smooth. Serve immediately.

Mangos, rich in belly-busting fiber, are an excellent source of vitamins A and C, as well as antioxidant flavonoids.

Aim to get at least 25 grams of fiber a day. Research shows that fiber may reduce the risk of death from cardiovascular disease.

Fiber can help decrease dangerous deep fat and abdominal fat, keeping you svelte and healthier.

Nutrients per serving:

Calories: 166
Total Fat: 2 g
Saturated Fat: 1 g
Trans Fat: 0 g
Cholesterol: 24 mg
Sodium: 63 mg
Total Carbohydrates 25 g
Dietary Fiber: 2 g
Sugars: 24 g
Protein 14 g
Iron 0 mg

Macronutrient Breakdown
60% Carbohydrates
30% Protein
10% Fat

Chocolate Cha-Cha

2 servings

ingredients

¼ to ½ cup (60 ml to 125 ml) unsweetened cocoa powder (choose amount depending on your preference for richer chocolate flavor)

1 cup (250 ml) nonfat milk

½ cup (125 ml) vanilla nonfat yogurt

1 teaspoon (5 ml) ground cinnamon

1 teaspoon (5 ml) freshly grated nutmeg

¼ teaspoon (1 ml) pure vanilla extract

Chocolate was first consumed as a beverage. The Maya prepared an unsweetened drink made from ground cocoa beans and spices.

Mexicans still add spices to their cocoa and chocolate.

steps

Process all ingredients in a blender until smooth. Serve immediately.

Nutrients per serving:

Calories: 128
Total Fat: 4 g
Saturated Fat: 2 g
Trans Fat: 0 g
Cholesterol: 4 mg
Sodium: 81 mg
Total Carbohydrates 13 g
Dietary Fiber: 8 g
Sugars: 11 g
Protein 10 g Iron 3 mg

Macronutrient Breakdown
41% Carbohydrates
31% Protein
28% Fat

Cocoa Loco

2 servings

ingredients

¼ cup (60 ml) unsweetened cocoa powder (choose amount depending on your preference for richer chocolate flavor)

1 cup (250 ml) coconut water

4 prunes

½ cup (125 ml) vanilla low-fat Greek yogurt

Stevia, to taste

The Aztecs and Maya used cocoa beans as currency.

Cocoa powder is one of the richest natural sources of flavanol, a naturally occurring antioxidant that is good for cardiovascular health.

Consuming cocoa powder and dark chocolate every day is linked with lowered blood pressure.

Coconut water is high in potassium, important for maintaining healthy blood vessels and blood pressure.

steps

Process all ingredients in a blender until smooth. Serve immediately.

Nutrients per serving:

Calories: 144
Total Fat: 3 g
Saturated Fat: 2 g
Trans Fat: 0 g
Cholesterol: 1 mg
Sodium: 153 mg
Total Carbohydrates 18 g
Dietary Fiber: 10 g
Sugars: 12 g
Protein 11 g
Iron 4 mg

Macronutrient Breakdown
51% Carbohydrates
30% Protein
19% Fat

Green Machine

2 servings

ingredients

½ cup (125 ml) baby spinach

½ cup (125 ml) kale

1 cup (250 ml) orange juice

½ tablespoon (7 ml) wheat germ

1 cup (250 ml) ice

steps

Process all ingredients in a blender until smooth. Serve immediately.

Eating a variety of leafy greens is a great way to get plenty of nutrients important for cardiovascular health.

Dietary guidelines recommend 2 cups (500 ml) of leafy greens a day.

Nutrients per serving:

Calories: 120
Total Fat: 2 g
Saturated Fat: 0 g
Trans Fat: 0 g
Cholesterol: 0 mg
Sodium: 15 mg
Total Carbohydrates 19 g
Dietary Fiber: 3 g
Sugars: 13 g
Protein 6 g
Iron 2 mg

Macronutrient Breakdown
65% Carbohydrates
20% Protein
15% Fat

Don't Break Your Heart

Berry Blast

2 servings

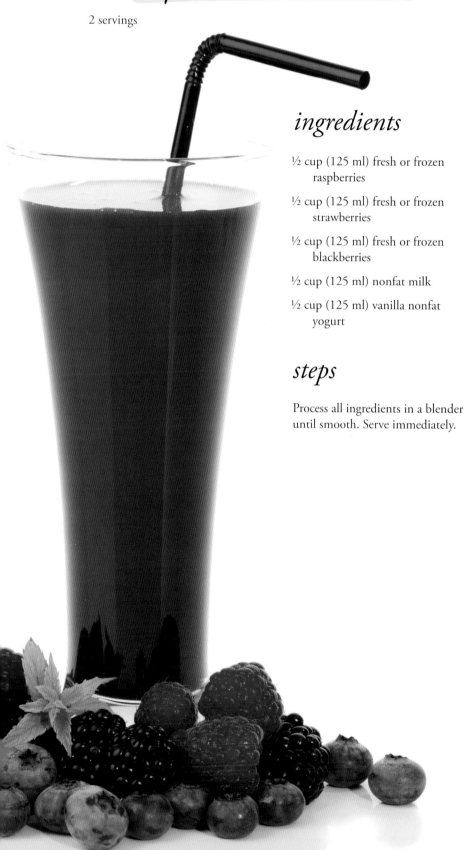

ingredients

½ cup (125 ml) fresh or frozen
raspberries

½ cup (125 ml) fresh or frozen
strawberries

½ cup (125 ml) fresh or frozen
blackberries

½ cup (125 ml) nonfat milk

½ cup (125 ml) vanilla nonfat
yogurt

steps

Process all ingredients in a blender
until smooth. Serve immediately.

*Berries rank as one of
the top antioxidant foods
because of their high
amounts of flavonoids and
vitamin C.*

*Flavonoids give berries their
rich red and purples hues.*

Nutrients per serving:

Calories: 92
Total Fat: 1 g
Saturated Fat: 0 g
Trans Fat: 0 g
Cholesterol: 2 mg
Sodium: 52 mg
Total Carbohydrates 16 g
Dietary Fiber: 5 g
Sugars: 12 g
Protein 5 g
Iron 1 mg

Macronutrient Breakdown
68% Carbohydrates
22% Protein
10% Fat

Strawberry Banana Original

2 servings

ingredients

1 banana

½ cup (125 ml) fresh or frozen strawberries

1 cup (250 ml) vanilla soy milk

2 tablespoons (30 ml) silk tofu

steps

Process all ingredients in a blender until smooth. Serve immediately.

Soy is one of only a few plant sources that contains high quality protein.

Nutrients per serving:

Calories: 128
Total Fat: 3 g
Saturated Fat: 0 g
Trans Fat: 0 g
Cholesterol: 0 mg
Sodium: 49 mg
Total Carbohydrates 20 g
Dietary Fiber: 3 g
Sugars: 13 g
Protein 5 g
Iron 1 mg

Macronutrient Breakdown
63% Carbohydrates
16% Protein
21% Fat

Blueberry Bliss

2 servings

ingredients

1½ cups (375 ml) nonfat milk

1 cup (250 ml) fresh or frozen blueberries

1 tablespoon (15 ml) low-sugar strawberry jam

1 tablespoon(15 ml) honey

1 cup (250 ml) ice

steps

Process all ingredients in a blender until smooth. Serve immediately.

Blueberries are rich in anthocyanins, flavonoids found to keep the brain sharp and prevent eye disease as you age.

Nutrients per serving:

Calories: 141
Total Fat: 0 g
Saturated Fat: 0 g
Trans Fat: 0 g
Cholesterol: 0 mg
Sodium: 78 mg
Total Carbohydrates 28 g
Dietary Fiber: 2 g
Sugars: 25 g
Protein 7 g
Iron 0 mg

Macronutrient Breakdown
80% Carbohydrates
20% Protein
0% Fat

Don't Break Your Heart

Kiwi Cocktail

2 servings

ingredients

4 kiwi fruit, peeled

1 cup (250 ml) frozen peaches

2 tablespoons (30 ml) honey

½ cup (125 ml) apple juice

2 cups (500 ml) ice

steps

Process all ingredients in a blender until smooth. Serve immediately.

A kiwi fruit contains more vitamin C than an orange.

Nutrients per serving:

Calories: 219
Total Fat: 1 g
Saturated Fat: 0 g
Trans Fat: 0 g
Cholesterol: 0 mg
Sodium: 8 mg, Total
Carbohydrates 50 g
Dietary Fiber: 6 g
Sugars: 44 g
Protein 3 g
Iron 1 mg

Macronutrient Breakdown
91% Carbohydrates
5% Protein
4% Fat

Antioxidant Powerhouse

2 servings

ingredients

1 cup (250 ml) shredded carrot

1 cup (250 ml) crushed pineapple

½ cup (125 ml) prune juice

1 cup (250 ml) vanilla low-fat yogurt

steps

Process all ingredients in a blender until smooth. Serve immediately.

Orange-colored fruits and vegetables are rich in beta-carotene, an antioxidant that helps keep free radicals from contributing to clots in blood vessels.

Nutrients per serving:

Calories: 175
Total Fat: 1 g
Saturated Fat: 0 g
Trans Fat: 0 g
Cholesterol: 2 mg
Sodium: 99 mg
Total Carbohydrates 37 g
Dietary Fiber: 4 g
Sugars: 30 g
Protein 5 g
Iron 1 mg

Macronutrient Breakdown
84% Carbohydrates
11% Protein
5% Fat

Don't Break Your Heart

Pumpkin Pleasure

2 servings

ingredients

1 cup (250 ml) pumpkin puree

1 cup (250 ml) nonfat milk

1 teaspoon (5 ml) ground cinnamon

1 tablespoon (15 ml) honey

2 cups (500 ml) ice

steps

Process all ingredients in a blender until smooth. Serve immediately.

Pumpkin, one of the richest sources of vitamin A, also contains lutein and zeaxanthin, two carotenoids that promote healthy eyes.

Nutrients per serving:

Calories: 118
Total Fat: 1 g
Saturated Fat: 0 g
Trans Fat: 0 g
Cholesterol: 2 mg
Sodium: 58 mg
Total Carbohydrates 21 g
Dietary Fiber: 4 g
Sugars: 19 g
Protein 6 g
Iron 2 mg

Macronutrient Breakdown
72% Carbohydrates
20% Protein
8% Fat

chapter 13

Divine Desserts

Sweet Truths

Anthocyanins, the deep red, purple, and blue pigments found in berries, help protect vessels from inflammation and plaque buildup.

Apple pectin, an antioxidant compound, helps shuttle cholesterol out of the body.

Dark chocolate and cocoa contain high amounts of flavanols, compounds that keep platelets from forming plaques in the arteries and that help with overall blood flow.

Nuts are rich in heart-healthy fat, minerals, and phytochemicals, all which help maintain a healthy cardiovascular system.

Featured Nutrients

The following nutrients in fruit-based and dark chocolate desserts provide energy and benefit overall health:

Vitamin C, fiber, magnesium, copper, folate, potassium, flavonoids, flavanols, anthocyanins, and nutrient-rich carbohydrates

Apples

An apple a day may indeed keep the doctor away. Studies show that apples, all natural applesauce, and even 100 percent apple juice can help lower the risk of developing heart disease and may also help decrease waist size and possibly even blood pressure. In one study adults who ate apples and apple products had smaller waistlines, less abdominal fat, lower blood pressure, and a reduced risk for developing metabolic syndrome—defined as having three or more symptoms related to heart disease risk, including elevated blood pressure, increased waist size, and elevated c-protein levels.

Pectin, a type of fiber found in plants, is especially concentrated in apples. Apple pectin binds to cholesterol in the gut and takes it out of the body. In one recent study, 160 women between the ages of 45 and 65 were divided into two groups. One group ate 75 grams of dried apple per day (about 2½ ounces), while the other ate an equal amount of dried prunes. The apple eaters experienced a 23 percent decrease in LDL "bad" cholesterol and increased their HDL "good" cholesterol by 3 to 4 percent.

Berries

Berries are rich in a variety of phytochemicals that help prevent diseases, including heart disease. Phytochemicals, compounds found in the pigments and skin of fruits and vegetables, provide plants with antioxidant protection against the stress caused by intense sunlight and rigorous growing conditions. In a similar way they protect human cells against internal stress that leads to cancer and heart disease.

One study found that women who consumed a few servings of strawberries each week were less likely to have elevations in C-reactive protein, an inflammatory marker associated with heart disease, in their blood. In addition, strawberries may lower the likelihood for bad cholesterol to oxidize and vessels to become inflamed. Both oxidation and inflammation can lead to heart disease.

Blueberries, raspberries, and blackberries are especially rich in flavonoids and ellagic acid, phytochemicals that can lower heart disease risk. In addition, they contain a significant dose of fiber, which helps remove cholesterol and keeps the blood flowing smoothly. Numerous studies show that diets rich in natural sources of fiber from fruits, vegetables, beans, and whole grains are protective of the heart.

Cocoa and Chocolate

Cocoa beans are rich in phytochemicals called flavanols. Studies show that flavanols contribute to heart health in several ways. For one, they reduce the tendency for platelets to stick together. Platelets are substances in the blood that can lead to plaque buildup in the arteries and blockages when they aggregate. Flavanols also contribute to the release of anti-inflammatory compounds, again helping reduce artery plaque buildup. Studies also find lower blood pressure and better cholesterol profiles (lower bad cholesterol and higher good cholesterol) in people who consume cocoa and flavanol-rich chocolates in their diets. Dark chocolates with 60 percent or higher cocoa are richer in the heart-healthy compounds than milk chocolates, which contain 35 percent or less cocoa.

The fat content in chocolates can be quite high, with more than 50 percent of calories coming from fat. However, it's worth noting that the majority of this fat is either monounsaturated fat, the healthy type found in olive oil, or from stearic acid. Stearic acid is a type of fat that's considered a saturated fat, but it doesn't raise cholesterol levels, the primary concern with saturated fats. Including small amounts of flavanol-rich chocolates can be a heart healthy practice. Studies find just 6 grams (about ¼ of an ounce) of dark chocolate a day can lower blood pressure. In addition, using natural cocoa powder in cooking or sprinkled over foods like yogurt or oatmeal is a low-fat way to add flavanols to your diet.

Nuts

Nuts are high in heart-healthy mono- and polyunsaturated fats. Eating 1½ ounces (40 g) of nuts a day, as part of a diet low in saturated fat and cholesterol, may reduce the risk of heart disease. Numerous studies show that nut eaters tend to have lower body weights and lower cholesterol counts. High in fiber, protein, and healthy fats, nuts are a well-balanced food that can and should be part of a healthy diet. Portion size is crucial with nuts because while they are full of nutrients, they are also calorie dense. Because chopped nuts add flavor and nutrition, you'll find them included in many of this book's recipes, deliciously paired with fruits and chocolate and sprinkled on salads.

Nut	Number in 1-ounce (15-g) portion size
Almonds	23
Brazil nuts	6
Cashews	18
Hazelnuts	21
Macadamia nuts	10 to 12
Peanuts*	42
Pecans	19 halves
Pine nuts	167 kernels
Walnuts	14 halves

*Peanuts are actually in the legume family but have a more similar fat profile to tree nuts. They are full of heart-healthy mono- and polyunsaturated fats. Study after study has linked a diet containing peanuts to lower cholesterol levels, healthier body weights, and cardiovascular protection. Peanuts contain protein, fiber, antioxidant phytochemicals, and phytosterols, which are compounds that help block cholesterol absorption in the body.

Winter Fruit Compote

4 servings

ingredients

1 cup (250 ml) apple juice

¼ cup (60 ml) packed light brown sugar

¼ cup (60 ml) water

1 tablespoon (15 ml) fresh lemon juice

½ cup (60 ml) dried apricot halves, quartered

½ cup (125 ml) dried whole figs, sliced

½ cup (125 ml) dried cranberries

½ teaspoon (2 ml) ground ginger

¼ teaspoon (1 ml) ground cinnamon

1 teaspoon (5 ml) pure vanilla extract

steps

1. Combine apple juice, brown sugar, water, and lemon juice in a small saucepan. Bring to a simmer and cook, stirring occasionally, until brown sugar is dissolved.

2. Add dried fruits and seasonings; simmer until fruits are plump, about 5 minutes.

Figs are a rich source of potassium and fiber, both of which help keep the cardiovascular system healthy.

With more than 150 varieties, figs vary in color from black-purple to green-yellow.

Figs have a long history as a sacred fruit, dating back to Greek and Roman times.

Nutrients per serving:

Calories: 224
Total Fat: 1 g
Saturated Fat: 0 g
Trans Fat: 0 g
Cholesterol: 0 mg
Sodium: 11 mg
Total Carbohydrates: 54 g
Dietary Fiber: 4 g
Sugars: 49 g
Protein: 1 g
Iron: 1 mg

Macronutrient Breakdown
94% Carbohydrates
2% Protein
4% Fat

(Served with 1 slice angel food cake)
Calories: 353
Total Fat: 1 g
Saturated Fat: 0 g
Trans Fat: 0 g
Cholesterol: 0 mg
Sodium: 266 mg
Total Carbohydrates: 81 g
Dietary Fiber: 4 g
Sugars: 64 g
Protein: 4 g
Iron: 1 mg

Macronutrient Breakdown
92% Carbohydrates
5% Protein
3% Fat

Chocolate-Dipped Dried Plums

12 servings (2 each)

ingredients

24 pitted dried plums

24 walnut halves

6 ounces (170 g) semi-sweet chocolate, coarsely chopped

steps

1. Cut a slit into the side of each dried plum. Stuff with a walnut half. Pinch to close; shape to form a ball. Set aside.

2. Place chocolate in a small heatproof bowl and set in a pot of hot, not boiling, water over low heat. Allow chocolate to melt, stirring occasionally, until smooth. Chocolate should be fluid and barely warm. Remove from heat.

3. Line a baking sheet with aluminum foil or wax paper. Using a fork, dip dried plums, 1 at a time, into chocolate; drain excess.

4. Place on the prepared baking sheet. Refrigerate until set.

5. When chocolate has hardened, transfer dried plums to jars or containers. Store, covered, in cool place, away from direct sun or heat.

Cooking Tip: Drizzle melted white chocolate over chocolate-dried plums or top plums with crushed nuts, if desired.

There are more than 2,000 varieties of plums.

Dried plums, or prunes, are high in sorbitol, an indigestible compound, which gives prunes their reputation for promoting regularity.

Nutrients per serving:

Calories: 141
Total Fat: 7 g
Saturated Fat: 3 g
Trans Fat: 0 g
Cholesterol: 0 mg
Sodium: 4 mg
Total Carbohydrates: 17 g
Dietary Fiber: 2 g
Sugars: 13 g
Protein: 2 fg
Iron: 1 mg

Macronutrient Breakdown
49% Carbohydrates
6% Protein
45% Fat

Fudge Pudding Cake

9 servings

ingredients

½ cup (125 ml) fat-free milk

¼ cup (60 ml) Dried Plum Puree (see below)

1 cup (250 ml) all-purpose flour

¾ cup (175 ml) granulated sugar

6 tablespoons (90 ml) unsweetened cocoa powder, divided

2 teaspoons (10 ml) baking powder

¼ teaspoon (1 ml) salt

1 cup (250 ml) packed light brown sugar

1½ cups (375 ml) hot water

½ cup (125 ml) light whipped topping

Like baking chocolate, cocoa powder is rich in antioxidant flavanols, but minus the fat.

steps

1. Preheat the oven to 350° F (180° C). Lightly coat an 8-inch (20-cm) square baking dish with nonstick cooking spray and set aside.

2. In a mixing bowl, beat together milk and Dried Plum Purée until blended thoroughly. Add flour, sugar, 2 tablespoons (30 ml) cocoa, baking powder, and salt; beat until just blended. Spread evenly onto the bottom of the prepared pan.

3. In a small bowl, combine brown sugar and remaining 4 tablespoons (60 ml) cocoa; sprinkle evenly over batter. Pour hot water over top. Bake for 45 minutes or until cake springs back when lightly touched. Cool for 15 minutes on a wire rack.

4. Cut into 9 squares; serve warm on individual plates. Top each square with even amounts of whipped topping.

Dried Plum Purée

Makes ½ cup (125 ml)

Ingredients

⅔ cup (150 ml) pitted dried plums

3 tablespoons (45 ml) water

Steps

In a food processor, combine dried plums and water. Process on and off until finely chopped.

Nutrients per serving:

Calories: 242
Total Fat: 1 g
Saturated Fat: 0 g
Trans Fat: 0 g
Cholesterol: 1 mg
Sodium: 166 mg Total
Carbohydrates: 54 g
Dietary Fiber: 2 g
Sugars: 44 g Protein: 3 g
Iron: 2 mg

Macronutrient Breakdown
91% Carbohydrates
5% Protein
4% Fat

Flavors-of-Fall Bread Delight

6 servings

ingredients

4 to 6 slices whole wheat bread, toasted

½ cup (125 ml) unsweetened applesauce

1½ cups (375 ml) shredded apple

1 egg, beaten

2 egg whites, beaten

2 cups (500 ml) nonfat milk

¼ cup (60 ml) granulated sugar

2 tablespoons (30 ml) pure vanilla extract

1 teaspoon (5 ml) ground cinnamon

½ teaspoon (2 ml) freshly grated nutmeg

steps

1. Preheat the oven to 350° F (180° C). Lightly coat an 8-inch (20-cm) square baking dish with nonstick cooking spray and set aside.

2. Place bread in the prepared baking dish.

3. Mix remaining ingredients together and pour over bread. Make sure bread is covered with liquid.

4. Cover with plastic wrap and refrigerate for 30 minutes.

5. Bake for 50 to 60 minutes.

Cooking Tip: Keep the skin on the apples, if desired. An apple with skin has twice as much fiber as one without.

Nutrients per serving:

Calories: 173
Total Fat: 2 g
Saturated Fat: 1 g
Trans Fat: 0 g
Cholesterol: 33 mg
Sodium: 175 mg
Total Carbohydrates: 31 g
Dietary Fiber: 3 g
Sugars: 20 g
Protein: 8 g
Iron: 1 mg

Macronutrient Breakdown
72% Carbohydrates
18% Protein
10% Fat

Don't Break Your Heart

Strawberry Trifle

6 servings

ingredients

⅓ cup (75 ml) granulated sugar

1 tablespoon (15 ml) cornstarch

2 large eggs

2 cups (500 ml) low-fat milk

1 teaspoon (5 ml) pure vanilla extract

6 (1-inch-thick) (5-cm-thick) slices angel food cake

¼ cup (60 ml) dry sherry

1 (16-ounce) (450-g) package frozen,
   sliced strawberries, thawed

6 tablespoons (90 ml) nonfat whipped topping, for garnish

2 tablespoons (30 ml) toasted sliced almonds, for garnish

steps

1. To make custard, whisk together sugar, cornstarch, and eggs in a bowl until smooth. Slowly whisk in milk. Transfer mixture to heavy-bottomed saucepan set over medium heat. Cook, whisking constantly, for about 5 minutes, or until mixture comes to a boil and thickens. Reduce heat to low; whisk for 1 minute more.

2. Remove from heat and whisk in vanilla. Transfer to a bowl; place a sheet of plastic wrap directly onto surface of custard. Refrigerate until chilled.

3. Place 1 slice angel food in the bottom of a 1-cup (250 ml) individual glass dish; sprinkle with 2 teaspoons (10 ml) of sherry.

4. Spread 2 tablespoons (30 ml) strawberries evenly over cake; spread ⅓ cup (75 ml) custard over strawberries. Top with 2 tablespoons (30 ml) strawberries; garnish with whipped cream and almonds.

Cooking Tip: Feel free to use either store-bought or homemade angel food cake with this recipe. Both are equally low in fat.

Nutrients per serving:

Calories: 290
Total Fat: 4 g
Saturated Fat: 1 g
Trans Fat: 0 g
Cholesterol: 66 mg
Sodium: 318 mg
Total Carbohydrates: 55 g
Dietary Fiber: 2 g
Sugars: 35 g
Protein: 9 g
Iron: 1 mg

Macronutrient Breakdown
76% Carbohydrates
12% Protein
12% Fat

Strawberry Cheesecake Bites

16 servings

ingredients

8 ounces (225 ml) Neufchatel reduced-fat cream cheese, softened

⅓ cup (75 ml) confectioners' sugar

2 teaspoons (10 ml) fresh lemon juice

½ teaspoon (2 ml) grated lemon peel

16 whole stemmed strawberries

8 low-fat graham cracker squares, finely crushed

One serving of 8 strawberries has more vitamin C than an orange.

steps

1. Beat together cream cheese, sugar, lemon juice, and lemon peel in a bowl until smooth and creamy; set aside.

2. Using a paring knife or a small melon baller, partially hollow out tops of strawberries to a depth of ¾ inch (1.5-cm). Gently fill each with 1 tablespoon (15 ml) cream cheese mixture.

3. Roll strawberries in graham cracker crumbs. Arrange on a serving platter.

Cooking Tip: To prepare recipe ahead of time, fill strawberries with cream cheese mixture, cover, and refrigerate up to 6 hours. Roll in graham cracker crumbs just before serving.

Nutrients per serving:

Calories: 65
Total Fat: 3 g
Saturated Fat: 2 g
Trans Fat: 0 g
Cholesterol: 10 mg
Sodium: 84 mg
Total Carbohydrates: 7 g
Dietary Fiber: 1 g
Sugars: 5 g
Protein: 2 g
Iron: 0 mg

Macronutrient Breakdown
46% Carbohydrates
12% Protein
42% Fat

Baked Apples with Banana-Date Filling

6 servings

ingredients

6 Jonagold or Golden Delicious apples, cored

1 large banana

1 tablespoon (15 ml) fresh lemon juice

2 tablespoons (30 ml) chopped dates

¼ cup (60 ml) chopped walnuts

2 tablespoons (30 ml) granulated sugar

½ cup (125 ml) water

¼ cup (60 ml) light corn syrup

½ lemon, sliced

Deglet Noor date, the most commonly consumed date in the United States, has a pleasing caramel-like taste.

steps

1. Preheat the oven to 350° F (180° C). Peel top third of apples and arrange, peeled end up, in a shallow baking dish. Peel and dice banana and sprinkle with lemon juice. Mix banana with dates, walnuts, and sugar. Spoon mixture into centers of apples.

2. Combine water, corn syrup, and lemon slices in a small saucepan and boil for 5 minutes. Pour liquid over apples. Bake, basting frequently with syrup, for 30 to 40 minutes, or until apples are tender.

Nutrients per serving:

Calories: 235
Total Fat: 4 g
Saturated Fat: 0 g
Trans Fat: 0 g
Cholesterol: 0 mg
Sodium: 12 mg
Total Carbohydrates: 48 g
Dietary Fiber: 7 g
Sugars: 36 g
Protein: 2 g
Iron: 1 mg

Macronutrient Breakdown
82% Carbohydrates
3% Protein
15% Fat

Apple-Rhubarb Napoleon

6 servings

ingredients

Pastry

1 extra-large egg white

1 teaspoon (5 ml) vegetable oil

2 tablespoons (30 ml) granulated sugar

2 tablespoons (30 ml) finely ground
   walnuts

¼ teaspoon (1 ml) ground cinnamon

6 (12- x 17-inch) (30- x 43-cm) sheets
   phyllo pastry, thawed

Filling

3 cups (750 ml) chopped fresh
   or frozen rhubarb

¾ cup (175 ml) granulated sugar

2 cups (500 ml) nonfat whipped or
   small curd cottage cheese

1 Granny Smith apple

Confectioners' sugar, for garnish

Rhubarb, a stem fruit resembling a pink celery stalk, is rich in fiber and potassium, both heart-healthy nutrients.

Since rhubarb is very tart raw, it's usually sweetened and added to pies or baked desserts.

steps

1. To prepare pastry, preheat the oven to 350° F (180° C). Coat 2 cookie sheets with nonstick cooking oil spray and set aside.

2. In a blender or food processor, combine egg white and oil and blend until well mixed. In a small bowl, combine sugar, walnuts, and cinnamon.

3. Place 1 phyllo sheet on a clean work surface. Brush lightly with egg white mixture, sprinkle with 2 teaspoons (10 ml) sugar mixture, then top with second sheet. Brush with egg white mixture and sprinkle with sugar mixture. Repeat layering with remaining 4 sheets, brushing and sprinkling each layer. Cut layered rectangle into 24 pieces. Transfer pieces to prepared cookie sheets and bake for 10 to 12 minutes, or until lightly browned. Set aside to cool.

4. Meanwhile, to prepare filling, combine rhubarb and ½ cup sugar (125 ml) in a saucepan set over medium-low heat. Cook, stirring occasionally, for 20 to 25 minutes, or until rhubarb is soft and chunky. Set aside to cool. In a blender or food processor, combine cottage cheese and remaining ¼ cup (60 ml) sugar; blend or process until cheese is smooth.

5. Just before serving, core apple and cut lengthwise into 24 pieces. In a microwave-safe dish, cover apple slices with waxed paper; microwave 35 to 45 seconds on high, or until softened. Cool slices.

6. To assemble each napoleon, place 1 piece phyllo on each of 6 serving plates. Top with 2 tablespoons (30 ml) cheese mixture, 1½ tablespoons (20 ml) rhubarb mixture, and 2 slices apple. Continue layering, using 2 more pieces of phyllo and the same amount of filling ingredients. Top with a final piece of phyllo, sprinkle with confectioners' sugar, and serve.

Nutrients per serving:

Calories: 284
Total Fat: 2 g
Saturated Fat: 0 g
Trans Fat: 0 g
Cholesterol: 5 mg
Sodium: 350 mg
Total Carbohydrates: 56 g
Dietary Fiber: 2 g
Sugars: 36 g
Protein: 11 g
Iron: 1 mg

Macronutrient Breakdown
79% Carbohydrates
15% Protein
6% Fat

Cinnamon Apple Wonder

6 servings

ingredients

1 tablespoon (15 ml) butter or margarine

¼ cup (60 ml) packed dark brown sugar

2 tablespoons (30 ml) ground cinnamon

3 Jonagold or Golden Delicious apples, peeled, cored, and thinly sliced

½ tablespoon (7 ml) pure vanilla extract

2 tablespoons (30 ml) fresh lemon juice

18 (12- by 17-inch) (30- x 43-cm) sheets phyllo pastry, thawed

The average American eats about 19 pounds of fresh apples annually, compared to about 46 pounds by a resident of a European country.

steps

1. Preheat the oven to 325° F (160° C). Melt butter in a large skillet set over medium heat. Stir in brown sugar and cinnamon. Add apples and cook until slightly softened. Add vanilla and lemon juice; cook until apples are tender. Cool to room temperature.

2. Place 1 sheet of phyllo on a clean work surface; lightly coat phyllo with nonstick cooking oil spray. Place a second sheet on top and spray again. Repeat with a third sheet. Cut stacked phyllo sheets crosswise into 6 equal strips.

3. Coat the inside of a custard cup or ½-cup (125-ml) ramekin with nonstick cooking oil spray. Place the end of one phyllo strip in the bottom of a cup, shaping it to the inside of the cup and leaving the other end extending over the edge. Repeat with remaining strips, overlapping them clockwise, in a circle around the cup with the inner ends stacked on the bottom. Fill the bottom with ½-cup (125 ml) apple mixture; pull overlapping strips together to form a "purse" when gathered together. Close with a light twist and then separate the strips above the twist for a fanned effect.

4. Repeat steps 2 and 3 to use remaining phyllo and apple filling, creating 5 more purses.

5. Bake for 15 to 20 minutes, or until lightly browned.

Nutrients per serving:

Calories: 300
Total Fat: 4 g
Saturated Fat: 1 g
Trans Fat: 0 g
Cholesterol: 5 mg
Sodium: 296 mg
Total Carbohydrates: 61 g
Dietary Fiber: 4 g
Sugars: 18 g
Protein: 5 g
Iron: 2 mg

Macronutrient Breakdown
81% Carbohydrates
7% Protein
12% Fat

Provençal Apple Spice Cake

8 servings

ingredients

1 cup (250 ml) cake flour, sifted

½ teaspoon (2 ml) baking powder

½ teaspoon (2 ml) ground allspice

¼ teaspoon (1 ml) ground cloves

2 large eggs

½ cup (125 ml) applesauce

½ cup (125 ml) packed brown sugar

3 tablespoons (45 ml) olive oil

1 teaspoon (5 ml) finely grated orange rind

1 Gala or Golden Delicious apple

Candied orange rind, for garnish (optional)

There are more than 7,500 varieties of apples worldwide.

steps

1. Preheat the oven to 350° F (180° C). Grease and flour an 8-inch (20-cm) round cake pan and set aside. In a medium bowl, combine flour, baking powder, allspice, and cloves; set aside.

2. In large bowl, beat eggs, applesauce, brown sugar, olive oil, and orange rind until well blended. Stir in dry ingredients, mixing gently, until combined.

3. Pour cake batter into the prepared pan. Peel and core apple; cut lengthwise into slices ¾-inch (2-cm) thick slices. Arrange slices in batter in a concentric circle like the spokes of a wheel. Bake until brown and firm, about 30 minutes.

4. To serve, invert pan to remove cake and place cake right side up. (This cake is sturdy and easy to handle.) If desired, garnish center of cake with candied orange rind.

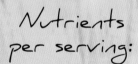

Nutrients per serving:

Calories: 199

Total Fat: 7 g

Saturated Fat: 1 g

Trans Fat: 0 g

Cholesterol: 47 mg

Sodium: 46 mg

Total Carbohydrates: 31 g

Dietary Fiber: 1 g

Sugars: 18 g

Protein: 3 g

Iron: 2 mg

Macronutrient Breakdown

62% Carbohydrates

6% Protein

32% Fat

Blueberry Clafoutis

8 servings

ingredients

2½ cups (375 ml) frozen blueberries

1 cup (250 ml) chopped walnuts

⅔ cup (150 ml) whole wheat flour

½ cup (125 ml) granulated sugar plus more for sprinkling

4 ounces (115 g) trans fat-free margarine

⅔ cup (150 ml) whole wheat flour

½ cup (125 ml) plus 1 tablespoon (15 ml) granulated sugar

2 large eggs

5 ounces (140 g) nonfat milk

1 teaspoon (5 ml) pure vanilla extract

1 tablespoon (15 ml) confectioners' sugar

Frozen blueberries are just as nutritious as fresh, and for most recipes you can use them right out of the freezer.

steps

1. Preheat the oven to 400° F (200° C). Coat 8 (6-ounce) (170-g) ramekins with nonstick cooking spray and sprinkle with sugar. Spoon equal portions of blueberries into the ramekins.

2. Grind ½ cup (125 ml) walnuts in a food processor. Add flour and sugar to ground nuts. Pulse to mix.

3. Heat margarine in a large saucepan until golden brown. Remove from heat. Whisk in eggs, milk, and vanilla. Fold in flour mixture. Spoon mixture over blueberries and sprinkle with remaining chopped walnuts.

4. Bake for 30 to 35 minutes. Let cool and sprinkle with confectioners' sugar. Serve lukewarm.

Nutrients per serving:

Calories: 320
Total Fat: 20 g
Saturated Fat: 3 g
Trans Fat: 0 g
Cholesterol: 47 mg
Sodium: 119 mg
Total Carbohydrates: 31 g
Dietary Fiber: 4 g
Sugars: 20 g
Protein: 8 g
Iron: 1 mg

Macronutrient Breakdown
34% Carbohydrates
10% Protein
56% Fat

Chocolate Almond Biscotti

16 servings

ingredients

3 large eggs

Grated peel of 2 oranges

1 teaspoon (5 ml) pure vanilla extract

½ teaspoon (2 ml) almond extract

1¾ cups (425 ml) all-purpose flour

⅓ cup (75 ml) unsweetened cocoa powder

¾ cup (175 ml) granulated sugar

1 teaspoon baking soda

¼ teaspoon (1 ml) salt

¾ cup whole almonds, toasted

Almonds are high in monounsaturated fats, the same fats found in olive oil that keep the bad cholesterol down.

Almonds are rich in vitamin E, an antioxidant that promotes cardiovascular health.

One handful of nuts a day decreases the risk for heart disease.

steps

1. Preheat the oven to 300° F (150° C). Coat a baking sheet with nonstick cooking oil spray and set aside.

2. In a small bowl, whisk together eggs, orange peel, vanilla, and almond extract.

3. In a large bowl, combine flour, cocoa powder, sugar, baking soda, and salt. Add egg mixture and mix just until blended. Stir in almonds.

4. Divide dough in half and form into logs about 12 inches (30 cm) long. Bake in the center of the oven, for about 50 minutes, until set and crisp around the edges. Remove to a wire rack and cool for 5 minutes.

5. Reduce heat to 275° F (135° C). Place logs on a cutting board and, with a serrated knife, cut on the diagonal into slices ½-inch (1-cm) thick. Lay slices flat on the prepared baking sheet, spacing slightly apart.

6. Return to oven and bake, turning once, until dry and lightly toasted, about 20 to 25 minutes. Place on racks to cool completely. Store in an airtight container.

Nutrients per serving:

Calories: 143
Total Fat: 5 g
Saturated Fat: 1 g
Trans Fat: 0 g
Cholesterol: 35 mg
Sodium: 93 mg
Total Carbohydrates: 21 g
Dietary Fiber: 2 g
Sugars: 10 g
Protein: 4 g
Iron: 1 mg

Macronutrient Breakdown
58% Carbohydrates
11% Protein
31% Fat

Chocolate Walnut Meringues

24 servings

ingredients

3 egg whites

Pinch of salt

¾ cup (175 ml) granulated sugar

½ cup (125 ml) good quality Dutch cocoa powder

⅓ cup (75 ml) finely chopped walnuts

steps

1. Preheat the oven to 350° F (180° C). Line a baking sheet with parchment paper and set aside.

2. Place egg whites and salt in a large stainless steel mixing bowl. Beat with an electric beater or by hand with a wire whisk until they form soft peaks.

3. Gradually add sugar until peaks stiffen.

4. Sift cocoa over peaks and fold in with walnuts.

5. Spoon mounds about 1 inch (2 cm) in diameter and about 1 inch (2 cm) apart onto the prepared baking sheet.

6. Bake for 20 minutes, or until dry to the touch. Let cool completely before removing from baking sheet.

Walnuts, rich in omega-3s called ALAs, promote heart health in a variety of ways. They reduce bad cholesterol and decrease platelet clotting and inflammation.

Walnuts are rich in magnesium and potassium, minerals that help maintain healthy blood pressure.

Nutrients per serving:

Calories: 41
Total Fat: 1 g
Saturated Fat: 0 g
Trans Fat: 0 g
Cholesterol: 0 mg
Sodium: 14 mg
Total Carbohydrates: 7 g
Dietary Fiber: 1 g
Sugars: 6 g
Protein: 1 g
Iron: 0 mg

Macronutrient Breakdown
68% Carbohydrate
10% Protein
22% Fat

Blueberry Crisp

6 servings

ingredients

4 cups (1 L) blueberries

¼ cup (60 ml) granulated sugar

½ teaspoon (2 ml) grated lemon rind

2 medium apples, peeled, cored, and diced

½ cup (125 ml) packed light brown sugar

2 teaspoons (10 ml) ground cinnamon

1 teaspoon (2 ml) freshly grated nutmeg

½ cup (125 ml) all-purpose flour

½ cup (125 ml) rolled oats

½ cup (125 ml) chopped pecans (optional)

3 tablespoons (45 ml) trans fat-free margarine

Blueberries have a high concentration of the flavonoid anthocyanin, a phytochemical found in blue-pigmented fruit.

steps

1. Preheat the oven to 325° F (160° C). Grease an 8- x 8- x 2-inch (20- x 20- x 5-cm) cake pan and set aside.

2. In a small bowl, combine blueberries, sugar, lemon rind, and apples and mix well. Place in the prepared pan. Combine brown sugar, cinnamon, nutmeg, flour, oats, and pecans, if using, in a medium bowl. Rub in margarine with your fingers until mixture resembles coarse crumbs. Spread evenly over blueberry filling.

3. Bake for 45 minutes, or until the crust is golden brown.

Nutrients per serving:

Calories: 302
Total Fat: 10 g
Saturated Fat: 1 g
Trans Fat: 0 g
Cholesterol: 0 mg
Sodium: 48 mg
Total Carbohydrates: 53 g
Dietary Fiber: 5 g
Sugars: 35 g
Protein: 4 g
Iron: 1 mg

Macronutrient Breakdown
65% Carbohydrates
5% Protein
30% Fat

Peanut Banana Bread

12 servings

ingredients

⅓ cup (75 ml) trans fat-free margarine

⅔ cup (150 ml) granulated sugar

1 egg

2 egg whites

½ teaspoon (2 ml) lemon extract

1¼ cup (300 ml) mashed, ripe bananas

1 cup (250) all-purpose flour

¾ cup (175 ml) whole wheat flour

2½ teaspoons (12 ml) baking powder

¾ cup (175 ml) coarsely chopped, unsalted, dry-roasted peanuts

White Tea Glaze (see page 29)

Peanuts, while consumed like nuts, are actually legumes and grow underground, not on trees.

In the United States, peanuts and peanut butter are the most popular nut choice and make up 67 percent of all nut consumption.

steps

1. Preheat the oven to 350° F (180° C). Grease a 9- x 5-inch (23- x 13-cm) loaf pan and set aside.

2. In a large bowl, cream together margarine and sugar with a mixer. Add eggs, lemon extract, and bananas. Mix well.

3. Sift together flours and baking powder.

4. Gradually add dry ingredients to banana mixture. Fold in peanuts.

5. Pour batter into the prepared pan. Bake for 60 minutes, or until golden brown.

6. Once cooled, drizzle with White Tea Glaze.

Nutrients per serving:

Calories: 254
Total Fat: 10 g
Saturated Fat: 2 g
Trans Fat: 0 g
Cholesterol: 18 mg
Sodium: 141 mg
Total Carbohydrates: 36 g
Dietary Fiber: 3 g
Sugars: 21 g
Protein: 6 g
Iron: 1 mg

Macronutrient Breakdown
56% Carbohydrates
9% Protein
35% Fat

Almond-Crusted Pumpkin Cheese Pie

16 servings

ingredients

1 cup (250 ml) whole almonds

2 tablespoons (30 ml) granulated sugar

1 cup (250 ml) gingersnap crumbs

⅓ cup (75 ml) trans fat-free margarine, melted

8 ounces (225 g) Neufchatel reduced-fat cream cheese

8 ounces (225 g) fat-free cream cheese

⅔ cup (150 ml) packed brown sugar

1 teaspoon (5 ml) grated orange peel

½ cup (125 ml) light sour cream

¾ cup (175 ml) egg substitute

1½ cups (375 ml) canned pumpkin

1½ teaspoons (7 ml) pumpkin pie spice

Rich in fiber, 1 cup of canned pumpkin has a mere 80 calories.

steps

1. Preheat the oven to 325° F (160° C). Spread almonds in a single layer on a cookie sheet and toast for 12 to 15 minutes until lightly browned. Cool; chop coarsely.

2. Place a generous ½ cup (125 ml) of almonds in a food processor with sugar. Using a metal blade, process until very finely chopped. Pour into a large bowl; add gingersnap crumbs and mix.

3. Pour in margarine and stir well to combine. Press into bottom and side of a 10-inch (25-cm) pie plate to form a crust.

4. Bake for 10 minutes; set aside to cool.

5. In a large bowl, beat reduced-fat and fat-free cream cheeses, brown sugar, and orange peel until well blended. Beat in sour cream and egg substitute until mixture is light and fluffy. Beat in pumpkin and pumpkin pie spice until well blended.

6. Place pie shell on a cookie sheet; pour pumpkin cheese mixture into crust.

7. Bake in the center of the oven for 45 minutes, or until filling is set. Let cool on a rack.

8. Cover and refrigerate overnight. Top with remaining chopped almonds and serve.

Nutrients per serving:

Calories: 217
Total Fat: 11 g
Saturated Fat: 3 g
Trans Fat: 0 g
Cholesterol: 11 mg
Sodium: 295 mg
Total Carbohydrates: 21 g
Dietary Fiber: 2 g
Sugars: 15 g
Protein: 8 g
Iron: 2 mg

Macronutrient Breakdown
39% Carbohydrates
15% Protein
46% Fat

Spiced Chocolate Almonds

16 servings

ingredients

1 large egg white

1 teaspoon (5 ml) pure vanilla extract

2 cups (500 ml) whole almonds

½ cup (125 ml) granulated sugar

¼ cup (60 ml) cornstarch

1 tablespoon (15 ml) unsweetened cocoa powder

1 teaspoon (5 ml) chili powder

¼ teaspoon (1 ml) kosher salt

½ teaspoon (2 ml) ground cinnamon

½ teaspoon (2 ml) ground cumin

About 1 ounce (25 g) of almonds contains as much calcium as ¼ cup (60 ml) of milk.

steps

1. Preheat the oven to 225° F (110° C). Line a baking sheet with parchment paper and set aside.

2. Place egg white in a large stainless steel bowl; whisk until frothy. Whisk in vanilla. Add almonds and gently toss until completely coated.

3. Place remaining ingredients in a bowl and toss until well combined. Add sugar mixture to the almonds, a quarter at a time, and gently toss until well coated.

4. Transfer almonds to the prepared sheet and arrange in a single layer. Bake for 15 minutes, stir, and bake for 15 more minutes, or until coating is lightly colored and dried out. Remove from oven and immediately loosen with a metal spatula. Cool before serving.

Cooking Tip: Serve these spicy almonds alone or mix them with 2 to 3 cups (500 to 750 ml) of popcorn.

Nutrients per serving:

Calories: 139
Total Fat: 9 g
Saturated Fat: 1 g
Trans Fat: 0 g
Cholesterol: 0 mg Sodium: 42 mg
Total Carbohydrates: 10 g
Dietary Fiber: 2 g
Sugars: 7 g
Protein: 4 g
Iron: 1 mg

Macronutrient Breakdown
30% Carbohydrates
12% Protein
58% Fat

chapter 14

Menu Plans

Now that you have these delicious recipes on hand, you can begin to incorporate them into your daily eating pattern. By making just a few adjustments to what you eat, you can increase the overall healthfulness of your diet.

The following menus will show you how easy it is to incorporate the recipes in this book to your diet. Notice the nutrition information at the bottom of each menu and use it to help plan your meals.

By gradually including our recipes into your day you can soon achieve a balanced diet within the healthful guidelines explained at the beginning of this book. Not only will your health benefit from the added incredible ingredients, your taste buds will enjoy the added flavor, zest, and variety, as well.

Menu 1

Breakfast

Oatmeal Pancakes with Berry Crush (page 129)

1 cup (250 ml) nonfat milk

coffee or tea, unsweetened

Lunch

Salmon Waldorf Salad (page 180)

1 medium pear

1 cup (250 ml) nonfat milk

Dinner

Alamo Chicken (page 108)

½ large baked sweet potato

½ cup steamed broccoli

Brown Rice Yeast Roll (page 141) with 1 teaspoon (5 ml) margarine

Snack

1 cup (250 ml) low-fat fruit yogurt

Chocolate-Dipped Dried Plums (page 253)

Nutritional information

Calories: 2390

Fat: 67 g (25%)

Sat Fat: 17 g

Protein: 118 g (20%)

Carbohydrates: 336 g (55%)

Fiber: 46 g

Menu 2

Breakfast

Sunny Breakfast Shake (page 228)
½ cup (125 ml) blueberries

Lunch

Black-Eyed Pea, Tomato, and Egg Salad (page 156)
6 ounces (170 g) nonfat Greek yogurt
1 cup (250 ml) green tea with
2 teaspoons (10 ml) sugar or stevia

Dinner

Grilled Salmon with Avocado Tarragon Sauce (page 81)
Oatmeal and Leek Risotto (page 131)
1 small apple
1 cup (250 ml) nonfat milk

Snack

10 baby carrots with Sun-Dried Tomato Hummus (page 158)
Winter Fruit Compote (page 252)

Nutritional information

Calories: 1663
Fat: 45 g (23%)
Sat Fat: 6 g
Protein: 95 g (23%)
Carbohydrates: 224 g (54%)
Fiber: 32 g

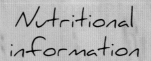

Menu 3

Breakfast

Southwest Lean Bean Scramble (page 168)

Cranberry Green Tea (page 214)

Lunch

Speedy Squash Soup (page 200)

Colorful Caprese Salad with Avocado (page 181)

Apple Barley Bread (page 140)

8 ounces (225 g) water

Dinner

Honey Pork Tenderloin Kebabs (page 42)

½ cup (125 ml) green beans

1 small baked potato with Edamame Avocado Dip (page 161)

Whole-Grain Corn Muffin (page 142)

1 cup (250 ml) nonfat milk

Snack

1 small apple

Spiced Chocolate Almonds (page 274)

Nutritional information

Calories: 1994

Fat: 51 g (23%)

Sat Fat: 13 g

Protein: 85 g (17%)

Carbohydrates: 302 g (60%)

Fiber: 41 g

Don't Break Your Heart

Menu 4

Breakfast

Peanut Butter Shake (page 229)

1 slice whole wheat bread

6 ounces (170 g) nonfat Greek yogurt

Lunch

Thai Chicken and Bean Wrap (page 169)

1 medium apple

Sunny Sips (page 218)

Dinner

Curry Beef and Aromatic Rice (page 54)

Black Bean, Lentil, Plantain Salad (page 155)

1 cup (250 ml) steamed broccoli

Baked Apples with Banana Date Filling (page 261)

1 cup (250 ml) nonfat milk

Snack

1 cheese stick

¼ cup (60 ml) dried cranberries

Nutritional information

Calories: 2196

Fat: 43 g (17%)

Sat Fat: 10 g

Protein: 128 g (22%)

Carbohydrates: 339 g (61%)

Fiber: 41 g

Menu 5

Breakfast

1 hardboiled egg with Tomato Cucumber Relish (page 166)

1 English muffin, toasted

1 cup (250 ml) nonfat milk

Lunch

Creamy Quinoa Pasta and Edamame Carbonara (page 132)

1 cup (250 ml) strawberries

8 ounces (225 g) water

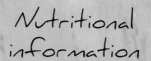

Dinner

5 ounces (140 g) grilled or steamed whitefish with Herbed Yogurt Sauce (page 29)

Sweet Potato with Baked Beans (page 154)

1 cup (250 ml) salad greens with

1 ounce (25 g) reduced-fat Cheddar cheese

1 tablespoon (15 ml) light vinaigrette salad dressing

8 ounces (225 g) water

Snack

½ cup (125 ml) low-fat cottage cheese

¾ cup (175 ml) pineapple

Nutritional information

Calories: 1764

Fat: 45 g (23%)

Sat Fat: 13 g

Protein: 121 g (26%)

Carbohydrates: 229 g (51%)

Fiber: 44 g

Menu 6

Breakfast

Sweet Potato Waffles/Pancakes (page 130) with ½ tablespoon (7 ml) maple syrup

6 ounces (170 g) nonfat Greek yogurt

coffee or tea, unsweetened

Lunch

3 ounces (90 ml) roasted chicken breast, boneless, skinless with Green Tea Rub (page 27)

Quinoa with Pesto (page 147)

1½ cup (125 ml) mixed vegetables, no salt added

8 ounces (225 g) water

Dinner

Turkey, Artichoke, and Tomato Tapas (page 114)

Apple Fennel Soup (page 202) with 5 whole-grain crackers

8 ounces (225 g) nonfat milk

Snack

Pumpkin Pie Pleasure (page 245)

1 grapefruit

1 medium pear

Nutritional information

Calories: 2196
Fat: 43 g (17%)
Sat Fat: 10 g
Protein: 128 g (22%)
Carbohydrates: 339 g (61%)
Fiber: 41 g

Acknowledgements

The authors would like to thank and acknowledge the following individuals and organizations for allowing them permission to use and/or adapt their wonderful heart-healthy recipes in this book:

Alaskan Seafood Marketing Institute (Salmon Waldorf Salad)

Almond Board of California (Almond-Crusted Pumpkin Cheese Pie; Chocolate Almond Biscotti; Spiced Chocolate Almonds)

Bob's Red Mill Natural Foods (Whole-Grain Corn Muffins)

California Dried Plum Board (Chocolate-Dipped Dried Plums; Fudge Pudding Cake)

California Strawberry Commission (Strawberry Cheesecake Bites; Strawberry Gazpacho; Strawberry Trifle)

Children's Hospital of Philadelphia (Flavors of Fall Bread Delight)

Clear Springs Seafood, Inc. (Grilled Trout Tacos with Pineapple Salsa)

Indian Harvest Specialty Foods (Whole Grains with Cranberries, Squash, and Pecans)

Joel Shaefer (Buckwheat Risotto with Goat Cheese)

King Arthur Flour Company, Inc. (Apple Barley Bread; Holiday Pumpkin Bread; Honey Wheat Rolls)

Meat & Livestock Australia (Australian Lamb Niçoise; Lamb Kabobs Wrapped in Pita)

MealMakeoverMoms.com (Festive Thai Shrimp; Grilled Salmon with Avocado Tarragon Sauce)

National Chicken Council (Alamo Chicken; Chicken Cutlet Salad with Strawberry Balsamic Dressing; Chicken with Golden Raisins; Green Olives and Lemons; Grilled Chicken Sandwiches with Pesto, Brie, and Arugula; Savory Chicken Primavera; Sweet and Spicy Tomato and Pepper Chicken Stew; Vietnamese Chicken Pho)

National Fisheries Institute (Honey Broiled Sea Scallops; Provençal Grilled Tuna Salad; Halibut with a Heart; Whole Wheat Crusted Tilapia)

National Pork Board (Asian Grilled Pork Tenderloin with Pineapple; Honey Pork Tenderloin Kebobs; Peachy Mustard Pork Chops; Rocky Mountain Soup; Thai Lettuce Wraps with Satay Pork Strips; Tuscan Pork and Bean Salad)

National Turkey Federation (Grilled Turkey Fajitas with Peach Salsa; Medallions with Chutney Sauce; Peppered Turkey; Tomato and Basil Turkey Bundles; Turkey and Avocado in Orange Sauce; Turkey, Artichoke, and Tomato Tapas; Turkey Breast with Honey Mustard Glaze)

Peanut Institute (Peanut Banana Bread)

Sarah Copeland; recipe adapted from her book The Newlywed Cookbook (Oatmeal Pancakes with Blackberry Crush)

Taste of Home (Brown Rice Yeast Rolls)

Texas Beef Council (Beef and Barley Vegetable Soup; Beef Mango and Barley Salad; Curry Beef and Aromatic Rice; Sirloin with Sugar Snap Peas and Pasta Salad; 30-Minute Beef Goulash)

Tuna Council and Chicken of the Sea (Change of Pace Tuna Casserole; Chunky Tuna Chowder)

U.S. Dry Bean Council (Baja Quesadillas; Black Bean Brownies; Black Bean and Walnut Burgers; Chicken, Bean, and Wild Rice Salad; Falafel; Sweet Onion and Apricot Limas; Thai Chicken and Bean Wraps; Turkey and Bean Salad with Apricot Ginger Dressing; Vegetable-Stuffed Peppers)

Veal Council (Honey Dijon Veal and Zucchini Stir-fry; Savory Veal Stew)

Washington Apple Commission (Apple Fennel Soup; Apple-Rhubarb Napoleon; Cinnamon-Apple Wonder; Baked Apples with Banana Date Filling; Provencal Apple Spice Cake; Speedy Squash Soup)

Whole Grain Gourmet (Sweet Potato Waffles)

Wild Blueberry Association of North America (Blueberry Baselito; Blueberry Clafoutis; Blueberry Crisp; Blueberry Soup; Blueberry Tomato Shooter)

Index

About the Authors

Shara Aaron, M.S., R.D., and Monica Bearden, R.D., are dietitians with years of experience communicating about health, wellness, and food, as well as researching the cardiovascular benefits of foods and beverages. In addition to teaching clients how to successfully lose weight and manage health conditions, Shara and Monica teach cooking classes, write articles and books, and regularly present to the public and other health professionals.

They co-wrote *The Baby Fat Diet* (Alpha, 2008) and *Chocolate – A Healthy Passion* (Prometheus, 2008) and regularly appear as guests on television, radio stations, and in print to discuss the health benefits of foods. The authors are owners of NutCom, LLC, Nutrition Communications, where they work with the food industry to help develop healthier products and then communicate the benefits of the products to health professionals and the public.

Shara and Monica blog and tweet regularly at www.babyfatdiet.com/blog and @babyfatdietRD, where they provide consumers with an understanding and context of the newest research in nutrition and food and keep in contact with readers and followers. View their portfolio at www.nut-com.com and contact them at nutrition@nut-com.com.